"In *Theology from the Psalms*, Professor C. H. Bullock presents a lifetime of scholarly study and pastoral reflection on the Psalms in short essays that nourish the soul and are delightful to read. What distinguishes this book are its careful attention to the Hebrew text, thoughtful bridges to Christian theology, and kindhearted tone. This book will give readers a deeper appreciation for the spiritual power and contemporary relevance of the Psalms. Anyone who preaches or teaches the Psalms will find treasures on every page that illuminate specific passages and a theological center of gravity that shows how the Psalter holds together."

—**Michael Graves**, author of *How Scripture Interprets Scripture*

"The Psalms have been an integral part of Hassell Bullock's personal and professional life for half a century (and more), and we, the readers, are the beneficiaries of this deep dive into the Psalter's theology. Rich and granular, engaging and stimulating, this book will reward anyone who dips into it, as they encounter topic after topic of the Psalms' theology, many not treated elsewhere. (How can one resist a book that has a chapter titled 'The Laughter of God'?) I recommend it enthusiastically!"

—**David M. Howard Jr.**, Bethlehem College and Seminary

"As Hassell Bullock writes, 'The book of Psalms' is basically 'Israel's theology compacted in one book.' From Bullock's lyrical and profound words opening the preface to his final meditations on how our present praise of God puts us in the rehearsal hall for eternity, *Theology from the Psalms: The Story of God's Steadfast Love* really does crown his forty years of studying, teaching, preaching, and writing on the Psalms. Read it, and be drawn into closer fellowship with God the Father, God the Son, and God the Holy Spirit."

—**Mark Talbot**, author of *When the Stars Disappear: Help and Hope from Stories of Suffering in Scripture*

"Concise, readable, and insightful! Bullock has done the academy and the church a service in writing a book that shows the rich theology of the Psalms. His masterful intertextual work demonstrates the scope and importance of the Psalms both then and now. Bullock's grasp of the ancient milieu of the Psalms and his seamless interaction with modern scholarship are commendable and make the work of the psalmists understandable and applicable for a modern aud'

an Neil Peterson, Lee University

"The rigor and warmth of Professor Hassell Bullock, well known to his students over decades of teaching, characterize the present volume. Drawing on a lifetime of close textual study of the Psalms, Bullock's work is rich in detailed observation and insight yet employs a theologically thematic outline that maintains an inviting accessibility. Readers of this volume will be welcomed to the text and challenged to engage it more carefully."

—Andrew Burlingame, Wheaton College

THEOLOGY
from the
PSALMS

THEOLOGY
from the
PSALMS

THE STORY
OF GOD'S STEADFAST LOVE

C. HASSELL BULLOCK

Baker Academic
a division of Baker Publishing Group
Grand Rapids, Michigan

© 2023 by C. Hassell Bullock

Published by Baker Academic
a division of Baker Publishing Group
Grand Rapids, Michigan
www.bakeracademic.com

Printed in the United States of America

Library of Congress Cataloging-in-Publication Data
Names: Bullock, C. Hassell, author.
Title: Theology from the Psalms : the story of God's steadfast love / C. Hassell Bullock.
Description: Grand Rapids, Michigan : Baker Academic, a division of Baker Publishing Group,
    [2023] | Includes bibliographical references and index.
Identifiers: LCCN 2023008935 | ISBN 9781540966964 (paperback) | ISBN 9781540967015
    (casebound) | ISBN 9781493443895 (ebook) | ISBN 9781493443901 (pdf)
Subjects: LCSH: Bible. Psalms—Criticism, interpretation, etc. | Bible. Psalms—Study and
    teaching. | Bible—Theology. | Bible—Commentaries.
Classification: LCC BS1430.52 .B86 2023 | DDC 223/.206—dc23/eng/20230530
LC record available at https://lccn.loc.gov/2023008935

Baker Publishing Group publications use paper produced from sustainable forestry practices and
post-consumer waste whenever possible.

23   24   25   26   27   28   29   7   6   5   4   3   2   1

To my dear grandchildren:
Ellen, Klara, and Lukas
Hannah and Matthew

CONTENTS

PART 3 REDEMPTION

PREFACE

Writing a theology of the Psalms is a task that draws the author and the reader into a three-thousand-year chain of life and history. Embraced in this chain are the psalmists themselves, along with the countless people who have found solace in their writings. The reasons for the powerful appeal of the Psalms are myriad, but most basically they speak to life in the real world, lived by real people, and they put people in touch with the real God who created them and loves them with a steadfast love.

This book is a product of more than forty years of teaching the Psalms in the college setting, thirty years of service to the church alongside my college ministry, and the capstone task of writing a commentary on the Psalms. We are all links in that continuing chain of writers and readers, like the saints in Hebrews 11, who by their faithfulness and God's wise design hold the chain together. Yet, there is something very humbling about our place and function in the chain. Some of the links are weak and others strong, but even the weak links benefit and find joy in the strength of others, while we confess with David, "I am poor and needy." Humility is a function of greatness.

When Baker gave me the privilege of writing a two-volume commentary on the Psalms (Teach the Text Commentary Series), I accepted it with the joy that, even after four decades of teaching the Psalms in the college classroom, I still had more to learn that I had not yet learned and more to say that I had not yet said. And that entailed working through all the psalms, one by one, in a depth that each psalm deserved and demanded. As I was fulfilling that task, at times it seemed overwhelming, but all along the Psalms were bidding me to "taste and see that the LORD is good" (Ps. 34:8). When I arrived at the challenging dark hues of Psalm 88, I was dealing personally with a life-threatening health crisis and an uncertain future, and I prayed with the psalmist, "You have put me in the depths of the pit, in the regions dark and deep" (88:6). In that experience, I recognized that I was not just studying this psalm, I was a living link in the chain. I was reminded of John Calvin's statement that we find God "in the fabric of the world."[1] Thankfully the Lord's steadfast love and abundant mercy "pursued" me to health again (23:6; see translation and discussion in "God's Love, the Shaper and Victor of History" in chap. 2), and with this new volume I am opening up further some theological vistas surveyed briefly in the commentary. And in some areas, I am hopefully advancing into new territory of thought and faith not surveyed at all in the commentary. My effort to articulate hermeneutical principles I have detected in the Psalms and then apply them as governing principles of this theology has, I believe, often shed new light and uncovered new depths in my understanding of these marvelous poems. Hopefully it will also provide some new and refreshing nuances to the readers of this book.

This theology, however, is not a compendium of conversations with other scholars and their critical views on the Psalms. Such exchanges appear in diminutive form from time to time, but this theology is a compilation of my own reflections on the Psalms, informed and even sometimes corrected by other authors and lovers of the Psalms. Part of the joy of writing this book has been the deep satisfaction of ruminating on the Psalms and hearing them speak to me in the strains of their writers and compilers with the assistance of the Holy Spirit. At the same time I am aware of the peril of private interpretations of Scripture, and especially those that close out all interpretive voices and listen only to their own. Such interpretations, however well intentioned, have sometimes summoned listeners to follow paths that do not lead to understanding our gracious God revealed in Jesus Christ. And that is the tragedy. In view of the many theological shipwrecks of spiritual leaders and their churches throughout my lifetime, over which I always grieve, I have come to pray daily the prayer of Psalm 69:6: "Let not those who hope in you be put to shame through me, O Lord GOD of hosts; let not those who seek you be brought to dishonor through me, O God of Israel."

A study of this nature, of course, owes a great debt to the myriads of voices that have prayed the Psalms and helped us hear God's voice through them.

---

1. Calvin, *Commentary on the Book of Psalms*, 4:146.

Such an exhaustive list cannot be compiled by us earthlings, for many of them are nameless and forgotten and among those "of whom the world was not worthy" (Heb. 11:38). And even if we could devise such a list, it would stretch around the planet several times. Yet, the God who knows every star and calls them all by name (Ps. 147:4) also has recorded the names of those worthies in his book of the living (69:28). So I will leave the review of this list to God as I give thanks for them all, named and unnamed.

Among those whose names I thankfully do know is my darling wife, Rhonda, number one on my list, who has stood patiently by me during the long composition hours, who loves the Psalms like I do, and who recites and sings them with me. Also high on the list are my students through the years—how can I say a thank-you worthy of their contribution to my studies and life! They have subsidized this theology by their words of encouragement, thoughtful questions, and their lives shaped by the Psalms, and heaven holds in waiting their sweet reward. Rabbi Hanina (second century AD) writes the script for me: "I have learned much from my teachers, and from my colleagues more than from my teachers, but from my students more than from them all" (Babylonian Talmud, Ta'anit 7a).

One of those students I must mention by name, now my trustworthy friend and interlocutor. Bryan Eklund has read this manuscript and commented out of his substantial knowledge of the Psalms, always stressing the spiritual heritage they bequeath to us, wherever our link in the chain may fall. Additionally, Dr. Michael Graves, Dr. Andrew Burlingame, and Dr. David Howard Jr., three of my former students, have volunteered, at my bidding, to write an endorsement of this volume. Knowing their academic integrity and commitment to excellence, I am confident that my professorial ego has not accentuated my "bidding" more heavily than their "volunteered." The two nonstudent endorsements are contributed by two senior scholars, Dr. Mark Talbot and Dr. Brian Peterson, with whom I have gratefully and profitably interacted from time to time through the years. Further, I thank Jim Kinney, Executive Vice President for academic publishing at Baker Publishing Group, who read this manuscript on one of his flights to a business meeting, saw its worth, and walked it through the approval process. Additionally, my gratitude goes to James Korsmo, senior editor—and I would add "extraordinaire" to that title—and the freelancers who work with him, who have lent their acute eye and quick wit to bring rhetorical precision to those places where it was lacking. Lastly, I mention among life's greatest blessings my children and their spouses, Scott Bullock and his wife, Britta, and Rebecca Sams and her husband, Michael. I still can see in my memory repository, scrawled in a child's hand in the margin of the *Scottish Psalter* at Psalm 23, "My favorite psalm." The psalmist affirmed this blessing best when he declared, "Children are a heritage from the LORD" (127:3), and in the next psalm prayed—I think for me and all others like me, who have lived to enjoy our grandchildren—"May you see your children's children!" (128:6). It is with deepest gratitude that I acknowledge the Lord's answer to that prayer on my and Rhonda's behalf. Taking my cue from there, I offer this book to God as a sacrifice of praise and dedicate it to my five grandchildren: Ellen, Klara, and Lukas Bullock, and Hannah and Matthew Sams. Someday I hope they will read this book, at least the preface, and fall more deeply in love with the Psalms and the Lord of the Psalms.

Soli Deo gloria!

Introductory Matters

Theology from the Psalms

The book of Psalms is unique among the books of the Bible in that it is an anthology of prayers and meditations collected from Israel's writings and worship experience over several centuries. At the same time, it is one of the most challenging books of the Old Testament for interpreters. Basically, it is Israel's theology compacted in one book. The anthological nature of the Psalms, with its contents stretched across the years, means in fact that we should wonder if a theology (singular) of the Psalms is even possible. My answer, in short, is in the affirmative. Not only does this book in its canonical form represent a multiplex of recensions, but behind that process is a theological filtering that has taken place under the scrutiny of Israel's spiritual forebears, most likely the priests and the prophets.

Some of the editorial processes that brought the book into existence and reshaped it from time to time, however elusive some of them may be, can still be detected. These processes admittedly are rather complex and have been discussed by numerous scholars, especially in the last century. For the most part, these editorial efforts are intended to give the book a particular perspective or, in some instances, to give portions of the book a particular perspective. I will consider two examples of an editorial recension intended to give the entire book a special perspective.

The first example is the shaping of David's portrait under the confession "I am poor and needy," which occurs four times in the book of Psalms (Pss. 40:17; 70:5; 86:1; 109:22). The initial indicator that this shaping effort was intentional can be detected from the fact that an unknown editor, perhaps the editor of this recension, picked up this confession from Book 1 (Ps. 40:17) and made it a vital part of the transition from Book 2 (Pss. 42–72) to Book 3 (Pss. 73–89), where David's personal profile from Book 1 transitions to Israel's corporate persona. Psalm 70:1–5 forms part of the transition to Book 3 by the quotation of 40:13–17 from Book 1 (see the excursus "An Analogy for the Editing Process of the Psalms" in chap. 10).

David is still King David, but he has assumed a second persona, the face of corporate Israel. The reuse of psalm material in another psalm is a standard editorial tactic in the Psalms. For example, Psalm 53 is a close duplicate of Psalm 14, and Psalm 108 borrows pieces of Psalms 57 and 60 to form its announcement of the "dawn" of a new era as the exiles in Babylonia experience renewed hope of returning home (108:6), all based not on human efforts that had been "worthless" (108:12 NIV) but on God's "steadfast love" and "faithfulness" (108:4). This profile alludes to Yahweh's revelation as "abounding in steadfast love and faithfulness" reflected in Exodus 34:6. The historical David in Psalm 40 engages in prayer against his mortal enemies (40:17), and in 70:1–5 David's persona is Israel. As my later discussion will show (see "David's Identification with His People: 'I Am Poor and Needy'" in chap. 6), this statement, "I am poor and needy," is the first formulaic occurrence of David's complaint about how his enemies have made his life miserable (40:17); the following three occurrences branch off from that initial confession. What the editor is seeking to accomplish is to paint the persona of David into the book so that ongoing generations of David's beloved Israel will know that he identified with them through their suffering and triumph and, in the fourth occurrence, that Yahweh was his *and* their Defense Attorney, standing at Israel's right hand to enable triumph over his *and* their enemies (109:31). The two personae, David and Israel, are intended to blend into each other. And it is not coincidental that David's confession occurs in four of the five books of the Psalms, and that all four psalms are attributed to David.

The second editorial endeavor intended to bring some theological uniformity to the book is the quotation of the second Sinai covenant (Exod. 34:6) in three different places, all three being David psalms. That is, David is confessing in the words Yahweh delivered to Moses. Moreover, this confession (called the "formula of grace")[1] occurs in anticipation of critical developments in

---

1. This is a commonly applied term to the contents of the second Sinai covenant (Exod. 34:6–7) that comprises Yahweh's self-description. When Moses had asked Yahweh to show him Yahweh's glory, Yahweh declined the request but promised that he would cause his goodness to pass by Moses, who was hidden in the cleft of the rock and could see Yahweh's back but not his

Israel's history. Occurring for the first time in 86:15 (Book 3), it anticipates the troubling theological disorientation that the end of the Davidic dynasty would thrust upon the nation (see 89:49). In anticipation of that tragic event brought about by the Babylonian conquest and reflected on in Psalm 89, David confesses his faith in the gracious God. When he asks, "Lord, where is your steadfast love of old, which by your faithfulness you swore to David?" (89:49), David has already answered the question by his confession of Exodus 34:6 in Psalm 86:15.

The second occurrence of this quotation occurs in the context of the nation's tragic exile to Babylonia with its calamitous consequences. In Psalm 103:8 (Book 4), David confesses his faith in the gracious God so the nation could see that Yahweh had not abandoned them, just as he had not abandoned his servant David. As one reads through the psalms of Book 4 in order there are hints of the exile and the new day on the horizon that awaits humiliated Israel. They paint a faint historical backdrop that can be too easily missed, even for astute readers of the psalms. Psalm 102:18–22 is an example that reflects the exile and the hope of a new people that will arise out of this great catastrophe:

> Let this be recorded for a generation to come,
>   so that a people yet to be created may praise the LORD:
> that he looked down from his holy height;
>   from heaven the LORD looked at the earth,
> to hear the groans of the prisoners,
>   to set free those who were doomed to die,
> that they may declare in Zion the name of the LORD,
>   and in Jerusalem his praise,
> when peoples gather together,
>   and kingdoms, to worship the LORD.

The third occurrence of the formula of grace (Ps. 145:8) is positioned in the final David psalm of Book 5. The nation, now delivered from exile, stands on the verge of the new age and anticipates the emergence of the kingdom of God, while David, for the final time in the Psalter, confesses his faith in the God of grace and mercy by quoting Exodus 34:6: "The LORD is gracious and

---

face. The term itself (in German, *Gnadenformel*) is used by Hermann Spieckermann in *Gottes Liebe zu Israel*, e.g., 10. I have not been able to identify the scholar who coined the phrase. For an in-depth study of the formula, see Hensley, *Covenant Relationships*.

merciful, slow to anger and abounding in steadfast love" (Ps. 145:8). Obviously, this recension of the book, like the "I am poor and needy" recension, is focused on David, Israel's greatest king, and points in the direction of the new era that is about to dawn (see 108:1–6) when the kingdom of David merges into the kingdom of God—when Yahweh, the real King of Israel, appears to reign over all his works:

> All your works shall give thanks to you, O Lord,
>   and all your saints shall bless you!
> They shall speak of the glory of your kingdom
>   and tell of your power,
> to make known to the children of man your mighty deeds,
>   and the glorious splendor of your kingdom.
> Your kingdom is an everlasting kingdom,
>   and your dominion endures throughout all generations. (145:10–13)

While the perception of a metanarrative in the Psalter poses a challenge for readers, there definitely is one that stands behind the poetic powers of the psalmists, particularly in the reference to historical events and persons and the innumerable allusions to such events and persons that are clear to the psalmists but less obvious to the readers.[2] Having recognized this distinctive feature of the metanarrative of the Psalms, we should understand that the two most worthy figures in the Psalter are Moses and David, and David is rendered in the persona of Moses by confessing his faith in the creed delivered to and confessed by Moses.

The two recensions of the book of Psalms discussed above are most likely major efforts to put Moses and David in a mutual alliance, based on their common faith, especially as written in the second Sinai covenant (Exod. 34:6–7). While these two recensions of the Psalter are rather easily recognizable, there were other recensions as well. Further, the smaller collections within the book show signs of introducing revisionist elements, for example, the Korah psalms (Pss. 42–49, 84–85, 87–88) and the Asaph Psalms (Pss. 50, 73–83).

There is much material written on the theology of the Psalms. Yet we should recognize, by the comprehensive nature of the Psalter itself, that any

---

2. Book 3 begins with a positive view of the temple (73:17), followed by explicit citations about the destruction of the temple (74:4–8; 79:1) and the end of the Davidic dynasty (89:3–4, 19–52; perhaps also 76:10), but never the kind of narrative that details the temple's destruction like we have in 2 Kings 25.

attempt to write a theology of the Psalms must proceed along the lines of a more or less comprehensive effort. That is, the enormous task will need to be defined and the limitations spelled out, or the task will never be finished. This, in fact, is the way we ought to look at a theology of the Psalms, a task that must be undertaken for God's sake and ours, but one whose last chapter will never be written, at least not in this world.

Not "Too Hard" and Not "Too Far Off"

When we approach the Psalms, our historical and theological knowledge of the Old Testament is definitely a plus factor for handling the book. That's what we bring to the book. But this mental database also proposes a challenge to allow the resources of the Psalms to inform us on Israel's history, theology, and culture. Ample information of these categories is definitely present in the book, and we can learn from that information. Of course, we need to be cognizant that the psalmic poets sometimes launch out on the authority of their poetic license and give us descriptions that are not in our biblical sources. For example, Psalm 105:16–18 describes Joseph's imprisonment in words that the Genesis text does not include (in italics):

> When he [Yahweh] summoned a famine on the land
> and broke all supply of bread,
> he had sent a man ahead of them,
> Joseph, who was sold as a slave.
> *His feet were hurt with fetters;*
> *his neck was put in a collar of iron.*

History, theology, and culture are often woven together in a way that requires the use of all our physical senses. While Moses's words in Deuteronomy 30:11–14 apply to Deuteronomy particularly, they are also a spiritual exhortation urging us to undertake the task of interpreting Scripture, and I suggest the Psalms are included:

> For this commandment that I command you today is not too hard for you, neither is it too far off. It is not in heaven that you should say, "Who will ascend to heaven for us and bring it to us, that we may hear it and do it?" Neither is it beyond the sea, that you should say, "Who will go over the sea for us and bring

it to us, that we may hear it and do it?" But the word is very near you. It is in your mouth and in your heart, so that you can do it.

In Deuteronomy 30 Moses particularly addresses Israel regarding the most trying and testing period of their history, exile from their homeland to foreign lands ("wherever the LORD your God disperses you among the nations," 30:1 NIV). Further, the book of Deuteronomy offers a review of Israel's memoirs to prepare them for those trying times, especially the Babylonian exile, and direct them back to the way of obedience, so they "return to the LORD your God, you and your children, and obey his voice in all that I command you today, with all your heart and with all your soul" (30:2). And Moses marks out the path of understanding God's word in general and dissuades God's people from thinking that it is too hard to understand. Indeed, those who are interested in God's word don't have to "ascend to heaven for us and bring it to us, that we may hear it and do it" (30:12), nor do they have to "go over the sea for us and bring it to us, that we may hear it and do it" (30:13). On the contrary, "the word is very near you. It is in your mouth and in your heart, so that you can do it" (30:14). The message is that God's word is readily available and accessible for Israel's and our understanding and obedience! It is also in this spirit that the Psalms should be read. They make accessible both orally ("in your mouth") and spiritually ("in your heart") life's difficulties, disappointments, and suffering in words that objectify them and in words that they, our spiritual forebears, and we, their spiritual beneficiaries, are often incapable of doing for ourselves.

An Anthology

Since the book itself is an anthology, a theology of the book will necessarily take an anthological approach. The compilers of the Psalter never intended to give it a systematic form, although I have chosen in the larger design of this book to follow a systematic outline—namely, God, humanity, and redemption. The chapters that fall under these three headings will be much more reflective of the anthological nature of the book than the systematic, and a topical approach serves the anthology well. Herman J. Selderhuis's *Calvin's Theology of the Psalms* is a commendable work based on John Calvin's *Commentary on the Book of Psalms*, and his systematic presentation of the Reformer's approach to the Psalms involves an admission that "the whole of his [Calvin's] theology as well as all of its parts constantly deal with God."[3] It would certainly be accurate to say the headwaters of the Psalms are Yahweh God, and the anthological nature of the Psalter, with its contents stretched across the centuries, gives us a picture of the tributaries that flow from the headwaters. It is a theology that is more inductive than deductive.

As I look at the Psalter, certain features suggest that the book is composed of layers that have overwritten others, not to create literary chaos but to enhance certain themes that the editors want to emphasize. In a later chapter I suggest the metaphor of a palimpsest manuscript, a written work that has been erased and written over (see the excursus "An Analogy for the Editing Process of the Psalms" in chap. 10). Sometimes the underlying writing is still faintly visible. We have modern technology that can even detect the writing that has been overwritten. We could conscript another metaphor and say that our infrared minds should scrutinize the Psalms for such an underscript. This is another way to speak of the editorial processes that have brought the book into existence and reshaped it from time to time. These processes are rather complex and have been discussed by numerous scholars, especially in the last century. For the most part, they are efforts to give the book or portions of the book a particular perspective.

A Bird's-Eye Overview

I have made a long list of topics that I would like to bring under the introspective power of my pen, and as I have launched the task, I have found that some topics ought to be merged and others subdivided. But what should the restraints look like? Included in this collection of essays are some topics that I have never seen treated in any collection of theological essays on these prayers and meditations, like "The Laughter of God," a topic that piques my own theological curiosity and, I believe, will spark an interest when readers see where I am going with it and why. Indeed, if Holy Writ can say of the Redeemer of the world, "he wept," why should its readers not look to the other side of the emotional spectrum to wonder if the Holy One—may his

---

3. Selderhuis, *Calvin's Theology of the Psalms*, 14. The English translation of Calvin's *Commentary on the Book of Psalms* is available in reprint by Baker.

name be blessed—ever laughs, whatever the motive. Since the Psalms speak about God's laughter three times, I believe the theme merits attention. By their very nature, of course, some chapters of this book will be shorter than others simply because they do not require the kind of detail or attention others do, or because a longer treatment would overload the topic or the book as a whole.

Obviously, the three theological centers of my outline—God, humanity, and redemption—interact and overlap, but the Psalter like the Bible in general is about God and sinful humanity. As indicated above, I believe, despite the elongated history of the collection, that the Psalter has a metanarrative—that is, a story that is deduced from the poetic material. The Psalms tell that story in its marvelous collection of laments, praises, and meditations.

Having concluded the introductory matters, I want to provide a bird's-eye view of parts 1, 2, and 3. While it will be most appropriate to read through this book in order, the anthological arrangement is such that readers may want to read some chapters before others.

Part 1 of the book is about God as he is revealed through the medium of the Psalms. Chapter 1 begins that conversation with a discussion of creation and redemption as two companion doctrines as they often appear in the Psalms and the importance of that combination to biblical theology. Chapter 2 sets forth the centrality of *hesed*, Yahweh's love, recognizing the kindred theme of God's love (*agapē*) in the New Testament. Chapter 3 recognizes the shared prominence of God's goodness in the creation narrative and the Psalms. Chapter 4 delves into Yahweh's condescension in the Psalter and the biblical doctrine of the incarnation. Chapter 5 seeks to open up the problem of the judgment of God over against justice and insist that the absence of judgment would render justice disqualified. Chapter 6 takes advantage of the prevalence of covenant in the Psalms and lays out the covenant platform on which the Old Testament is built and on which the Psalms are also secured. Chapter 7 investigates the trifold mention of God's laughter in the Psalms.

Part 2 shifts attention to humanity and the sinful nature that separates humanity and God. Chapter 8 inquires about the human condition, perverted by sin and in desperate need of redemption. Chapter 9 focuses on the nature of idolatry and makes a case for idolatry being the original sin. Chapter 10 investigates the frequent language about shame and its function in Israel's world. Chapter 11 recognizes the psychological tendency in the ancient world to speak in opposites, such as sorrow and joy. Chapter 12 investigates the spiritual virtue of waiting on the Lord. Chapter 13 takes a look at the perplexing imprecatory psalms and proposes a perspective that may help to redeem those psalms for theology, if such redemption is necessary.

Part 3 turns to the capstone of psalmic theology, the place where God and humanity meet with one another, based not on humanity's sinful and rebellious ways but on God's steadfast love. Chapter 14 explores the meaning of the peculiar phrase "for his [Yahweh's] name's sake," proposing a family or covenant setting for it. Chapter 15 deals with the reality that humanity finds God in the fabric of everyday life, one of the absolutely beautiful features of psalmic theology. Chapter 16 explores the multifaceted meaning of the spiritual posture described as "the fear of the Lord," exploring its dimensions as the earthly plateau of Israel's and our relationship to Yahweh. Chapter 17 makes a case for the Psalms as a teaching instrument for the praise of God, praise that is preparatory for the eternal praise of God.

Reflecting on Methodology

In this study I am attempting to duplicate, at least to a degree, the methodology of the psalmists themselves, because I believe their methodology is one of the reasons the Psalms have thrived as an instrument of worship and comfort through the centuries. First is the psalmists' practice of putting their message in both literal and metaphorical language, and I will follow their lead in the effort to understand that message, paying attention to the literary and rhetorical methods that constitute their poetry. Message and literary method, by the very nature of the written word, are inseparably linked.

Second, the psalmists addressed the issues of their times, bringing their wisdom and the Scriptures of the Hebrew Bible to bear on these issues, both personal and national (the use of the Hebrew Scriptures will be discussed below). As a member and minister of Christ's church, I cannot afford to do less, though I cannot claim the psalmists' infallible authority. Nevertheless, my attempt to employ the tested and proven hermeneutical methods of the Christian church and the Jewish interpreters through the centuries will always be uppermost in my methodology, even when I am applying the psalms to today's cultural and moral issues.

Third, the literary structure of many of the psalms is inseparably linked to message, and it will be my aim to show how they lean on each other to deliver and enhance that message. If readers are not accustomed to this mutual dependence, perhaps they will need to linger over these passages more patiently and give those texts a chance to prove themselves.

Fourth, the Psalms incorporate the Hebrew Scriptures, sometimes quoting but most often alluding to other Old Testament texts.[4] This feature, often referred to as "intertextuality," has in recent years become a subdiscipline of its own and is applied to other books of the Old and New Testaments as well. This feature of Psalms studies, in my view, issues a mandate that we should give attention to the way the Hebrew Scriptures are used.[5] The mandate, as I interpret it, includes the liberty to range broadly in the Hebrew Scriptures, which I will do unapologetically. Beyond that, since I write as a Christian believer, the mandate at the same time authorizes us to seek the fuller sense of psalmic theology in the Christian gospel. Even though our intertestamental methodology may sometimes seem overwrought in its attempt to "messianize" the Psalms, especially all of them, we must still read many of them as a template for a corresponding New Testament doctrine, such as the incarnation of God in Christ, true God and true Man,[6] and perhaps come closer to understanding how the New Testament writers arrived at their application. This methodology is an approximate equivalence to the typological method of interpreting the Old Testament. So my incursions into Christian theology will be received, I hope, with the recognition that they are my effort to facilitate our understanding of the Psalms and realize Moses's assurance that they are, like his own retelling of Israel's story in Deuteronomy, an assurance that "the word is very near you. It is in your mouth and in your heart, so that you can do it."

This task to write a theology of the Psalms, reflecting similar methodologies to those of the psalmists, is a challenge, but I believe its final benefits will reward the effort. Further, the assurance of Moses that God's word is readily available to our understanding is an encouragement to expect this effort to be assisted by a power that not only is beyond our earthly capabilities but is the real power that enables our interpretation of Holy Scripture.

---

4. See the excursus "Psalm 8 and the Image of God" in chap. 9.

5. See, e.g., my interpretation of "a little lower than God" (Ps. 8:5) as an allusion to the "image of God" in Gen. 1, in chap. 1, "The *Aleph* and *Tav* of Psalmic Theology."

6. See chap. 4, "Yahweh's Condescension in the Psalter," in which I present the humbled Yahweh and the exalted Yahweh of the Psalter to be a template on which the New Testament doctrine of the incarnation of God in Christ, true God and true Man, can and ought to be viewed.

The Phenomenal Privilege of Prayer

The topic of prayer has been much discussed and its practice much employed in the history of God's people. In Calvin's *Institutes of the Christian Religion*, his chapter on prayer is the longest chapter of all. Herman Selderhuis says Calvin "prayed much because he expected so much from it."[7] P. T. Forsyth, recognizing the mysterious power of prayer, says that writing on prayer is as awesome as touching the ark.[8] Forsyth's simile is enough to remind me that I should approach this topic with reverence and caution, and if the "oxen stumble" (2 Sam. 6:6–7), as they did on that fateful occasion in David's day, I shouldn't reach out to steady the ark.

Personal prayer is one of the noble privileges of God's children, a gift of grace beyond comparison. We can individually have an audience with the Creator of the universe and the Redeemer of the world, and he listens to us! In fact, our prayers are precious in God's sight. He bids us come and commune with him, to have a private conversation with our Creator, who freely offers grace to the world he made. Indeed, he is eager for us to accept the invitation. In human terms, we can say that God can hardly wait to hear us pray. Isaiah puts it into memorable words: "Before they call I will answer; while they are still speaking I will hear" (Isa. 65:24). And that was in contrast to a people who had the opposite reaction when the Lord came to them: "For when I called, no one answered, when I spoke, no one listened" (Isa. 66:4 NIV).

Two Basic Models of Prayer

Contrary to a modern critical view of the Psalms (that they are overwhelmingly written for the corporate worship in the temple, even the psalms that are composed in the first person "I," a view I'll discuss under "The Power of Corporate Prayer" below), there are many psalms that arise out of personal circumstances and express the individual's sentiments. They came into being in the crucible of personal troubles and anxieties and were not necessarily intended to be congregational prayers, even though some of them were adapted for that purpose. So we should anticipate that while the "I" of the Psalms is frequently the personal "I" of the writer and the nation's voice is articulated

7. Selderhuis, *John Calvin*, 161.
8. Forsyth, *The Soul of Prayer*, 37.

as "we," the personal "I" is also often the corporate "I," the voice of Israel as the nation prays.

Prayer has many engagement models, but I would like to speak about two of the basics, personal and corporate prayer, each of which could be reduced to a plethora of subdivisions. One of those subdivisions, intercessory prayer, for example, is a model that shares a claim on both. It can be corporate and personal. The content of prayer, of course, can vary with the individual or the congregation that prays, but prayers of praise, lament, petition, thanksgiving, and meditation are standard types of prayer. Perhaps meditative prayer is one that we might least expect to see in the list of types, but in reality many of the psalms are examples of that kind of prayer.[9] It would be more accurate to say that meditations, like praise and lament and so on, are more likely to constitute part of a psalm than characterize the whole psalm.

God listens to his people even when they are meditating on his goodness in their lives, and the Korahites, gatekeepers of the temple, meditate on God's love: "We have thought on your steadfast love, O God, in the midst of your temple" (Ps. 48:9).

Psalms are personal when they are made by an individual with the intention of interceding with God on one's own behalf, or buoying someone else above their pain and doubt, sometimes when they can't reach that level of intercession for themselves. Psalms are corporate, indeed the corporate voice of Israel and the voice of Christ's church, when two or more voices join together in a common concern. The intercessors do not necessarily become proxies, taking the place of that person for whom the prayers are made, but they engage in an act of intercession that functions in the same way as Jesus described the work of the Comforter in John 16:7, where the Greek word is *paraklētos* and means "one who comes alongside" us. The intercessor "comes alongside" the person for whom the prayer is made.

Paul engages the notion of corporate prayer in Romans 15:30 when he invites the Roman church to join with him in his struggle by praying for him: "I appeal to you, brothers, by our Lord Jesus Christ and by the love of the Spirit, to strive together with me in your prayers to God on my behalf." Paul was in effect inviting them to do what he admonished the Galatians to do: "Bear one another's burdens, and so fulfill the law of Christ" (Gal. 6:2). The "law of Christ" was an operating principle of the kingdom of Christ. In this

9. E.g., Ps. 4; see also Bullock, *Psalms*, 1:24.

instance, bearing another's burden may not be an absolute substitution but an associate relationship, supporting a person in his or her anguish and trouble. That is what Paul is inviting the Roman Christians to do, to enter his struggle, not to become his total struggle-bearer but to be his associate in bearing up under his struggle. They became "associates in prayer," and the experience was very real because through prayer they had entered into his struggle. This entry into someone else's dilemma and taking their personal need as one's own is at the heart of intercessory prayer. We not only share the knowledge of their need but take it upon ourselves as a personal privilege to pray for them. It does not necessarily mean that we must sleep on the stone floor to identify with our friend in prison, but who can rule that out as one's sense of personal identity with the object of our prayers!

The other side of this transaction is Christ reaching out to us and offering to bear our burdens, as he does in Matthew 11:28–30. In the context of a prayer to his heavenly Father, the Lord Jesus bids his disciples to "come to me, all who labor and are heavy laden, and I will give you rest. Take my yoke upon you and learn from me, for I am gentle and lowly in heart, and you will find rest for your souls. For my yoke is easy and my burden is light." In this case, Christ becomes our associate in prayer, making our burdens "light" because he is helping us bear them. Christ is not saying that he bears our burdens so we won't have to, although that vicarious function certainly takes its place as the absolute and ultimate function of God's redeeming grace in Christ (Isa. 53:4–6; 1 Pet. 2:24–25). Involved in this Matthew text is the idea that Christ is sometimes our helper rather than our surrogate. Underlying this view of redemption is that Christ is also our teacher, helping us to learn something about ourselves and our own situation rather than taking the burden and becoming our proxy in that circumstance. At the same time we learn something about Christ, about his love and constant presence to help us. We learn, informed by Hebrews 7:25, that Christ prays for us: "Consequently, he is able to save to the uttermost those who draw near to God through him, since he always lives to make intercession for them." So we gain understanding from both perspectives.

The Power of Corporate Prayer

There are many places in the Psalms where the singular personal pronoun "I" is intended to be more inclusive than the individual psalmist who is writing. The pronoun includes the whole congregation/nation of Israel. This is especially true in Book 5 of the Psalter (Pss. 107–50), perhaps because the nation is celebrating its miraculous return from exile and the people are rebuilding their temple and their life. In Hermann Gunkel's monumental work on the Psalms, he insisted that the "I" of the Psalms was sometimes corporate, inclusive of the larger congregation of Israel.[10] His protégé Sigmund Mowinckel took this idea to another level,[11] understanding virtually all the personal I's of the Psalter to be corporate. This meant that the book of Psalms was a prayer book crafted for the congregation, particularly for temple worship, with very few psalms that arose from a personal social context. This was quite a departure from the way the book had been viewed historically, seeing and using the psalms as personal prayers and meditations, while also recognizing they had been and should be used as instruments of the corporate prayers of the synagogue and church. Erhard Gerstenberger, on the other hand, insists, and I believe correctly, that the "prayer book of Israel" thesis was a bit overdrawn.[12]

Admittedly, in ancient Israel the psychology of personhood was strongly corporate—the individual existed for the sake of the community but not just for the community, for there was also a strong and robust individualism. An example is Job, whom Yahweh singles out and whose faith he puts to the test. While the individualism of Israel's world was nothing like we have in the Western world today, it was nevertheless one that still recognized the individual person's worth and considered the individual as the basic social unit. Yet, the relationship between these two views of personhood was much more balanced than in our modern world. Some of the psalms, in fact, give evidence of that more balanced perspective. Either the psalmist or a later editor thought that a corporate perspective was needed to make the very personal psalm complete. Psalm 25:22 illustrates this and functions as an addendum to the psalm. It recognizes that the psalmist's personal prayer for forgiveness (e.g., "Remember not the sins of my youth or my transgressions," v. 7) could not be complete until Israel as the corporate unit was forgiven and redeemed and turns the light onto that view of the individual/corporate relationship: "Redeem Israel, O God, out of all his troubles." I believe we could profit greatly by learning from this hybrid model of personhood.

As we have already observed, the use of the corporate "I" is especially prominent in Book 5 of the Psalter (Pss. 107–50)—the whole nation is praying.

10. Gunkel, *Introduction to Psalms*.
11. Mowinckel, *The Psalms in Israel's Worship* and *He That Cometh*.
12. Gerstenberger, *Psalms*, 33.

Since it was collected against the background of the return from Babylonian captivity, it is understandable that the psalmists of Book 5 speak collectively in many of the prayers and meditations of Book 5, and sometimes the pronoun "I" is even a hybrid of the personal and corporate—both are intended.

Corporate Prayer in Psalms 116 and 118

Psalms 116 and 118 can serve as illustrations of the hybrid personhood model. Written in the first-person-singular "I," obviously by an individual, and composed in the context of the return from exile (ca. 536 BC), Psalm 116 expresses the individual's suffering in exile, which was also the exiled people's suffering: "The cords of death entangled me, the anguish of the grave came over me; I was overcome by distress and sorrow" (Ps. 116:3 NIV). But the psalmist also rehearses the Lord's goodness, quite likely to be identified with the return from exile to the promised land, which verse 9 calls "the land of the living": "Return, O my soul, to your rest; for the LORD has dealt bountifully with you" (v. 7). And the celebrant contemplates what he/Israel can do to honor the Lord properly for his goodness: "What shall I render to the LORD for all his benefits to me?" (v. 12). The response is that he vows to call a service of thanksgiving to celebrate with the Lord's people: "I will lift up the cup of salvation and call on the name of the LORD, I will pay my vows to the LORD in the presence of all his people" (vv. 13–14). As the suppliant contemplates his vows of thanksgiving—that is, to hold a service of thanksgiving—he also remembers the precious saints (*hasidim*, v. 15), likely those who had died in the exile and would not be gathering in the new temple for the special service of thanksgiving.

The great service of thanksgiving is outlined in Psalm 118, where it is quite clear that the nation is speaking ("Let Israel say," v. 2), affirming the corporate nature of the "I" of this psalm. Quite beautifully, the voices of Psalm 118 form an ensemble: the voices of Moses (Ps. 118:14 = Exod. 15:2), David (Pss. 118:5; 31:8), the celebrant (Ps. 118:1, 29), the nation (Ps. 118:2), and the priests (Ps. 118:3, 26–27)—like Exodus 15, the whole nation is speaking. It is certainly worth noting that the voice of Moses is a quotation from the Song of Moses (Exod. 15:2), celebrating Israel's deliverance from Egypt as they were now celebrating their deliverance from the second exile (Babylonian captivity): "You have loosed my bonds" (Ps. 116:16).[13] No one would deny that the Song

---

13. Bullock, *Psalms*, 2:349–50.

of Moses was a song to be sung by corporate Israel, and the use of Exodus 15:2 here in Psalm 118:14 suggests the corporate worship of God's people. We might say that the psalmist looks at his life in exile and deliverance from captivity in a parabolic way. As is often the case with the psalmists, they see themselves as reliving the life of their ancestors, both individually and corporately. The capstone of the psalm is the psalmist's confession in the words of Israel's formulaic confession of Yahweh as their God: "You are my God" (Ps. 118:28). We should recall that the exile was the time when Israel gave up their idolatry, once and for all, and embraced Yahweh as their God (see chap. 9, "We Become Like Our God").

The fact that Psalm 118 is a corporate psalm and that it leans in the direction of Psalm 116 suggests that the individual psalmist of Psalm 116 was praying both as an individual *and* as the nation whose voice(s) clearly resounds in Psalm 118.

Two Functions of Corporate Prayer

There is a peculiar power in corporate prayer, not because God regards the prayers of the community of faith more than he does the prayers of the individual, but because there is unity in corporate prayer, a unity of purpose and petition, and God honors that unity (Ps. 133:1). Several times in Solomon's prayer of dedication of the temple he refers to Israel's prayers with the clause "when/if they pray toward this place" (1 Kings 8:30, 35; cf. 8:44, 48). These were their individual prayers combined into a petitionary chorus before God, united in a single purpose. Our prayers as a church on behalf of our common concerns represent the body of Christ and also contribute to the unity of his body, for he prayed "that they all may be one, just as you, Father, are in me, and I in you" (John 17:21). In corporate prayer the church unites, portending the glorious unity of the body of Christ when the story of redemption is recorded in the final chapter of saving grace (see Rev. 19–22). The Chronicler affirms the power of corporate prayer in his account of the dedication of the temple by inserting the Lord's promise: "If my people who are called by my name humble themselves, and pray and seek my face and turn from their wicked ways, then I will hear from heaven and will forgive their sin and heal their land" (2 Chron. 7:14). A nation cannot repent vicariously through the repentance of one or two individuals (Ezek. 14:13–14). It requires all of God's people to pray with a united voice and singular purpose. When the church in Jerusalem prayed for Peter in prison, the Lord miraculously loosed his shackles, and Peter appeared a free man before the praying church ("but earnest prayer for him was made to God by the church," Acts 12:5).

Thus corporate prayer has at least two functions. First, it unites God's people in a singular purpose and petition, and God is attentive to the united prayers of his people. Second, coming together with a singular purpose, formulated in a single petition, corresponds to the unity of the Father and the Son, which is the ultimate goal of the Spirit of God as we are brought into intimate fellowship with God (John 17:11, 20–26). It is certainly not an overstatement to say that God is moved by his people's prayers. That's the way he has set up the relationship, and it is not so much the power of prayer as it is the power of grace!

The Pinnacle of Grace

Yet the power of grace proceeds to one higher level, which we might call the pinnacle of grace, where, in the words of Isaiah, that ancient prophet of divine mystery and mercy, God becomes our substitute and bears our burdens for us. The prophet Isaiah laid out that idea before Paul did and made it part of the divine platform of grace, that the Suffering Servant "has borne our griefs and carried our sorrows" (Isa. 53:4). Yet the apostle informs us that the "Spirit intercedes for God's people," suggesting that it is a much larger enterprise than our personal and corporate situations, even bigger than our prayers (Rom. 8:27 NIV). As Augustine prays so beautifully, "O omnipotent Good, you who care for each one of us as though he was your only care and who cares for all of us as though we were all just one person."[14]

---

14. Augustine, *The Confessions of St. Augustine*, book 3, chap. 11 (pp. 66–67).

PART 1

GOD

ONE

The *Aleph* and *Tav* of Psalmic Theology

Creation and Redemption in Dynamic Relationship

As we have already acknowledged, there is a dynamic relationship in the Psalms between the two doctrines of creation and redemption. The simple reason is that the one God is both Creator and Redeemer. We can even say that the DNA of redemption is written in the story of creation. The defining terms of creation are spelled out in the book of Genesis: God made the world, including all living creatures, whose functions he also determined. Humanity, distinguished as male and female, made in the image of God, is the crown of the eight works in the entire cycle of creation in Genesis 1. Moreover, the story of creation is shaped in such a way as to make a character statement about the Creator. The two creation narratives are complementary in this respect. The Creator God of Genesis 1 speaks and it comes to pass, giving us an image of the *transcendent God*. He speaks, even speaks to humanity (Gen. 1:28–30), but his human creatures never speak to him. In the creation narrative of Genesis 2, however, there is interaction between the Lord God and Adam. The Lord God is very much a hands-on deity, forming the man from the dust of the ground and interacting with the man and woman—he is the *immanent God*. In a general sense, these two portraits of God become the underlying view of God portrayed in Scripture: God is both transcendent and immanent and will always be known as a God who interacts with his human creatures. It is in both the transcendence and immanence of the Creator God that redemption's story unfolds. There is no better source in the Old Testament for this profile of our Creator and Redeemer God than the Psalms, and the design and content of this study are intended to demonstrate some of the major dimensions of this portrayal.

God's Steadfast Love (*Hesed*), the Underlying Motive

Sometimes we miss important movements in the Psalms for various reasons; either we are inattentive, or we are looking for some specific idea and pass over another important one, or a plethora of other reasons. In the case of Psalm 136, for example, the refrain "for [or "because"] his steadfast love endures forever"[1] is a theological "pearl of great price," much like John 3:16, opening a priceless window into the character of God. Psalm 136:4–9 reviews the wonders of creation and lines each wonder with the refrain "*for* [or "*because*"] his steadfast love endures forever."[2] The truth that interpreters sometimes miss is the fact that the refrain is not merely for liturgical purposes, but that one little word "because" (*ki*) drives home the truth that God's steadfast love is the underlying reason for both creation and redemption. The same is true of the long list of redemptive events that constitute 136:10–25. Thus the golden tether of God's steadfast love connects all the pieces of Israel's creation and redemption history.

The Language of Creation

While the verbal and nominal terms of creation and redemption occur many times in the Psalms, here we are speaking about those verbs and nouns as well as the broader rhetorical phenomena that—absent the topic-specific terms—still proclaim the wonders. For example, except for the nominal form "my redeemer" in Psalm 19:14, the specific language of creation and redemption does not occur in Psalm 19. Yet, part 1 of Psalm 19 (vv. 1–6) sings an oratorio of creation: "The heavens declare the glory of God" (v. 1), and in part 2 (vv. 7–14) redemption is the theme: "The law of the LORD is perfect, refreshing the soul" (v. 7). Part 1 celebrates the transcendent God who brought

---

1. The NIV chooses not to translate "for/because" (*ki*), leaving the reader, especially the non-Hebrew reader, oblivious to this detail.

2. Italics in Scripture quotations have been added for emphasis.

the masterpiece into being, and part 2 celebrates the immanent God who gave the torah for the purpose of redemption. It could be considered a theological cover piece for Genesis 1–3. Our suppliant knows this relationship as an inseparable union, and he can pray with abandon, "Let the words of my mouth and the meditation of my heart be acceptable in your sight, O LORD, my rock and my redeemer [*go'ali*]" (Ps. 19:14).

When I speak of creation in this study, I make reference primarily to the physical world as we know it, including all the living creatures, humanity being the crowning work of the created order. Psalm 19 is the classic representative of the voice of creation itself declaring God's glory. God gave creation a voice, and it sings his glory in its disciplined and quiet movements. The psalmists have splendid ways of describing creation, sometimes reflecting the creation account itself (e.g., "he spoke," Pss. 33:9; 148:5 ["he commanded;"[3] "he spoke" in Gen. 1 carries the sense of "command"]; cf. Gen. 1:3, etc., "and God said," same Hebrew verb), and in other instances introducing their own poetic terms for creation (e.g., Ps. 8:5, "a little lower than God" (author's translation, hereafter AT),[4] poetic equivalent of "the image of God" (Gen. 1:27). In a superbly beautiful hymn, Psalm 114:3–6 uses personification to weave a tapestry of grace out of God's redeeming acts in history. A compact story of Israel's redemption, Psalm 114 portrays creation itself as an admiring observer of the miracles at the (Red) sea and the Jordan River, and as an ecstatic eyewitness to Israel's entry into Canaan (the mountains and hills). The truth that the personification delivers, much like Psalm 19:1–6, is that the creation is gripped by the awe and wonder of God's redeeming work. And that wonder elicits all creation's awe of the presence of the Lord:

> Tremble, O earth, at the presence of the LORD,
>   at the presence of the God of Jacob,
> who turns the rock into a pool of water,
>   the flint into a spring of water. (Ps. 114:7–8)

3. This is an excellent place to see how well the writer of Ps. 148 understood the "and God *said*" of Gen. 1. He knew that it carried the force of a command, and that is the way he rendered it.

4. The Greek translation, which the KJV and many English translations follow, has "angels" (*angelous*), which is the translator's way of rendering the Hebrew "God" (*'elohim*). It is likely that the translator did not want to associate "God" with the diminutive phrase "a little lower than," so he substitutes "angels" for "God." The clause was the psalmist's way of rendering the Hebrew phrase "image of God." See the excursus "Psalm 8 and the Image of God" in chap. 9.

The Language of Redemption

The description of redemption in the Psalms is much more complex than the language of creation. As already indicated, redemption is widely inclusive, encompassing God's work of maintaining the created order, especially order in the human family. This involves what we commonly refer to as providence. Two verbs in the Psalms cover the semantic range of "redeem," *g'l* and *pdh*. The first, *g'l*, occurs 118 times in the Old Testament and 11 times in the Psalter, including two occurrences of nominal forms. Its ground-level usage has to do with the legal functions of family and community life, regulating the Sabbath year (Lev. 25:1–7), the year of Jubilee (Lev. 25:8–17), and the more prosperous Israelites' care of their impoverished kin and neighbors (Lev. 25:23–55). In this last regard, the redeemer (*go'el*) was the more prosperous Israelite who redeemed the economically and socially disadvantaged. The function of redemption in this context had to do with ransoming someone who was in trouble or in poverty; the closest of kin had the responsibility of redeeming that person.

EXCURSUS: BOAZ THE "REDEEMER" (*GO'EL*)

The book of Ruth gives us the story of a couple, Elimelech and Naomi, who leave Bethlehem because of a famine and move to the country of Moab. After Naomi's husband dies, and then also her two sons who had married Moabite women, Naomi hears that the famine has subsided in Bethlehem, and she decides to return. Ruth, the more persistent of Naomi's daughters-in-law, accompanies her to Bethlehem despite Naomi's encouragement for her to stay in her own country. Once Naomi is back home, the patrimonial property of her deceased husband is by law subject to sale to the next of kin, called the redeemer (*go'el*). Boaz addresses this man, unnamed in the narrative, by a nondescript title (*peloni 'almoni*, Ruth 4:1), which is equivalent to "what's-your-name" or "so-and-so." Since neither of Naomi's two sons had survived, the rights of redemption of her husband's property pass down the family line to the next closest of kin. Boaz is second in line, and he carries out his responsibility at the city gate to convene the town court and puts the first-rights recipient on the spot. While obviously able to pay the unstipulated price of the property, the man refuses when he learns that Ruth has to be part of the bargain—that is, he must marry her. Thus the legal right-of-property passes on to Boaz.

The second verb, *pdh*, has a wide semantic range. It too has legal implications at the ground level of its usage, one of the examples being the redemption (*peduyim*, from the root *pdh*) of the firstborn male children and their substitution by the Levites (Num. 3:40–51). Firstborn males belong to the Lord, but the Israelites were allowed to pay a certain sum to "redeem" their firstborn sons. The exchange of something for equal value is the economic principle involved in the idea of redemption, although the same legal usage is not evident in the Psalter. For the most part, the two verbs for "redeem" tended with time to lose their legal overtones. And to our benefit, by the power of grace, when Yahweh is used as the subject of either verb in the Psalms, there is no exchange value involved. While we should not fill in the blanks for the psalmists when they give no clear directive, it is nevertheless quite appropriate for Christians to recognize that Jesus Christ as the exchange value of our redemption—no, an incomparable value—is acknowledged by our New Testament faith. As I have mentioned elsewhere in this study, sometimes rather than a clear messianic prediction, the Psalms supply only the template[5] on which the New Testament writers spell out the vicarious sacrifice of Christ. Isaiah, the closest theological associate the book of Psalms has in the Old Testament, certainly spells out this truth clearly (Isa. 53:4–6). Paul proffered the same theology in his Corinthian correspondence: "God made him who had no sin to be sin for us, so that in him we might become the righteousness of God" (2 Cor. 5:21 NIV).

Creation and Redemption Conjoined in the Psalms

The Oratorio of Creation and Redemption (Ps. 19)

As already noted, Psalm 19 is an excellent illustration of how the two doctrines of creation and redemption are conjoined in the Psalter. A second feature

---

5. I am using the term "template" to suggest that there is an organic relationship between certain doctrines of the Old Testament and corresponding doctrines in the New Testament. While the idea of predictive prophecy is certainly a valid hermeneutical method, there are some New Testament doctrines, like the incarnation, that are, in my opinion, better understood by viewing the Old Testament as a template on which the New Testament doctrine builds. That is not to deny that a text like Isa. 7:14 is a direct prophecy of the incarnation. Sometimes this phenomenon may be referred to as progressive revelation. I believe that even the Psalms provide a template on which the incarnation of God in Christ is laid, allowing us to see the organic development as God "breathed into" Scripture. The doctrine of the incarnation, so beautifully and clearly laid out in John 1, basically appears on the template of David's portrait (e.g., Ps. 110:1). See chap. 4, "Yahweh's Condescension in the Psalter."

of the psalm, the use of the divine names, supports the observation that part 2 is a minor oratorio on redemption.

First, we should note that we can often discern more acutely the meaning of a psalm text by observing the divine names used by the author. In part 1 (vv. 1–6) the divine name *'el*, the shortened form of *'elohim,* is used; this is the name of God that is used in the creation account of Genesis 1—the transcendent God. The covenant name LORD God (*Yahweh 'elohim*) governs part 2 (vv. 7–14)—the immanent God. The God who made the world—the transcendent God—redeems it through the power of the torah, through which Yahweh, the immanent God, forgives sins (vv. 12–13). The psalmist even uses the verb "to rule over" (*mshl*, v. 13), which the Lord used to inform Cain that he must "rule over" sin (Gen. 4:7). Finally, the psalmist uses the participle *go'el* (redeemer) to conclude the psalm: "O LORD, my rock and my redeemer [*go'ali*]" (Ps. 19:14).

Before we proceed further, we should, secondly, say something more about the nature of redemption in the Psalter. Here we may profitably draw from the Heidelberg Catechism to help us understand the broad-ranging nature of redemption as the psalmists spell it out. The simple structure of the catechism falls into three parts, which, I would insist, cover quite well the psalmic nature of redemption: Part I: Misery; Part II: Deliverance; Part III: Gratitude. The catechism is arranged according to the 52 Lord's Days and treats the three topics with a series of 129 questions and answers:

Part I: Misery (Q&A 2–11: Lord's Days 2–4) deals with our sins, using the hendiadys "sins and miseries."

Part II: Deliverance (Q&A 12–85: Lord's Days 5–31) deals with the realities of redemption.

Part III: Gratitude (Q&A 86–129: Lord's Days 32–52) presents the human response to redemption.

The catechism asks, "What is your only comfort in life and in death?" (Q. 1). It answers that it is knowing that we are not our own but belong to Christ, who has made full satisfaction for all our sins by his precious blood (A. 1). Then the catechism asks, "What must you know to live and die in the joy of this comfort?" (Q. 2). It answers, "Three things: first, how great my sin and misery are; second, how I am set free [redeemed] from all my sins and misery; third, how I am to thank God for such deliverance"

(A. 2). Question 2, in fact, presents the outline of the whole Catechism: Misery, Deliverance, and Gratitude. It is a brilliant teaching instrument, and, I suggest, a helpful way to look at the Psalms, particularly the story of redemption.

Second, what the catechism calls "sins and misery" is our fallen condition, which the Psalms know so well and describe so acutely in a myriad of ways, though they never relate the story of the fall as we read it in Genesis. Obviously, the term "sins" is no surprise to us, nor would it have been to the psalmists, but the term "misery" may be a surprise because we think of this term largely in emotional tones. In the contextual world of the Psalms, the lament psalms often cover the spectrum of knowing how great are our sins, which the Catechism labels as "Misery," expressive of living in this world in alienation from God. Additionally, Israel's bondage in Egypt is among the historical situations to which the verb *pdh* applies (Deut. 7:8; 9:26; etc.; Ps. 78:42). Other human circumstances—such as sickness, oppression, social injustice, false accusations, wicked schemes, and death—are among the objects of redemption.

Third, while the Psalms are not ordered in a systematic way, the Catechism, I suggest, is a mirror of the theological concerns of the psalmists. In the Psalms the terms *g'l* and *pdh*, generally speaking, are the verb functions of divine deliverance, even though the verb *pdh* only once takes "sins" as its object (Ps. 130:8). We may again draw upon the Heidelberg Catechism to assist our understanding of redemption as laid out in the Psalms. As we have already acknowledged above, the term "misery" covers those conditions that divine providence redeems, a doctrine the catechism spells out so well:

Q. 27. What do you mean by the providence of God?

A. 27. The almighty and everywhere present power of God, whereby, as it were by His hand, He upholds and governs heaven, earth, and all creatures; so that herbs and grass, rain and drought, fruitful and barren years, meat and drink, health and sickness, riches and poverty, yea, and all things come, not by chance, but by His fatherly hand.

In the Psalms, God's "fatherly hand" or "right hand" is a frequent metaphor for his redeeming work, and the psalmists are keenly aware of that gracious truth.

Creation and Redemption Bound with God's Steadfast Love (Ps. 33)

A similar conjunction of these two great doctrines is visible in Psalm 33, where the psalmist again ties together creation and redemption with the golden tether of God's steadfast love (*hesed*). After the opening verses, our poet declares that "the earth is full of the steadfast love of the LORD" (v. 5), then describes the creation of the world (vv. 6–9), and follows that with a longer description of redemption that includes the Lord's foiling the plans of Israel's enemies, the Lord's watchful care of his own people, and the futility of Israel's effort to save themselves (vv. 10–22).

Noted at the end of the redemption pericope is the Lord's watchful care of "those who hope in his steadfast love, that he may deliver ("redeem" [*ntsl*]) their soul from death and keep them alive in famine" (33:18–19). Here we have a neat literary feature that occurs in other psalms, where the psalmist structures the poem to illustrate his theological message. In this case, it is the use of the inclusio, introducing the Lord's "steadfast love" (*hesed*) in verse 5 ("The earth is full of the steadfast love of the LORD") and closing the inclusio at verse 22 ("Let your steadfast love, O LORD, be upon us"). In between, the psalmist also employs "steadfast love" (*hesed*) in verse 18 to reinforce the inclusio, suggesting the threadlike character of God's steadfast love that runs through the psalm and through life itself. Further, to authenticate the description of creation, the psalmist uses the terms of Genesis 1 (spirit, heavens, sea, deep, earth), and the text even reflects the grammatical terms of that story ("he spoke" [*'amar*]; "it came to be" [*wayehi*]), confirming the creation connection.

Creation and Redemption Celebrated (Pss. 65–66)

Psalms 65 and 66 are complementary psalms. Psalm 65 celebrates in hybrid form the doctrines of creation (65:5–8) and redemption (65:9–13),[6] and Psalm 66 celebrates redemption (66:5–20), particularly redemption from Egyptian

---

6. While these verses celebrate creation, they are also about the ongoing renewal of creation or providence, which is a category of redemption. See Paul's statement on the futility of creation and its "groaning together in the pains of childbirth until now" (Rom. 8:18–25). Sin has infected the created order. In fact, Isaiah intimates that infection and its redemption when he uses the metaphor of the child leading the ferocious lion and bear: "The wolf shall dwell with the lamb, and the leopard shall lie down with the young goat, and the calf and the lion and the fattened calf together; and a little child shall lead them" (Isa. 11:6). While we have to be cautious that we do not overinterpret metaphors, Isaiah, it seems to me, sees the estrangement between the animal and human worlds and views the correction of that relationship as the proper restoration of universal peace.

bondage (v. 6, "He turned the sea into dry land; they passed through the river on foot") and the victory of Canaan (v. 12, "a place of abundance"). As we have observed above, all of God's works on Israel's behalf, historically and personally, were redemptive works, laying the template for the great work of redemption in Jesus Christ that God had planned for Israel and humanity from the foundation of the world (1 Pet. 1:19–20). The promise to fulfill the vows the psalmist has made to God (Pss. 65:1; 66:13) points in the direction of a service of thanksgiving, and the emphasis upon the agricultural abundance with which God has blessed Israel (65:9–13) may suggest more generally the category of the agricultural festivals rather than a specific one (Passover/Unleavened Bread—barley harvest; Weeks—wheat harvest; Tabernacles—grape harvest). The thanksgiving service was voluntary, and the suppliant celebrated it in the temple with family and friends.

Psalm 66 is a microcosm bursting with God's redemptive work: first, all the earth, all humankind (vv. 1–4; "Shout for joy to God, all the earth," v. 4); second, Israel, who invites even the "peoples" to join them in the praise of God for the exodus from Egypt (vv. 5–12; "Come and see what God has done. . . . He turned the sea into dry land," vv. 5–7); and third, the psalmist (v. 16; "Come and hear, all you who fear God, and I will tell what he has done for my soul"). The pattern is the world, Israel, and the individual. Reinforcing this pattern is the fact that God is directly addressed three times in the psalm: once by "all the earth" (vv. 3–4); once by Israel (vv. 10–12), and once by the psalmist (vv. 13–15). This three-tiered model of redemption is a witness to the comprehensive program of redemption attested in the Psalms and fulfilled in the Christian gospel. We might note that, as often is the case in the Psalms, the psalmist's witness to God's actions on behalf of his people (vv. 5–12) prompts, at least in part, the psalmist's vows to celebrate God's deliverance. This can be seen in the fact that the psalmist moves without interruption from the rehearsal of what God has done for his people (vv. 5–7) and for the peoples outside of Israel (vv. 8–12) to his own vows to celebrate what God has done for him in a service of thanksgiving (vv. 13–15). The service of thanksgiving, in fact, is recorded in summary in verses 16–19: "Come and hear, all you who fear God, and I will tell what he has done for my soul." This is a good illustration of the concept of hybrid personhood in ancient Israel, which was constituted by a delicate balance of the corporate identity with personal identity.[7]

7. For this model of personhood, see "The Power of Corporate Prayer" in "Introductory Matters."

The Creator-Redeemer God in the Nooks and Crannies of the Universe (Ps. 139)

It is not unusual in the Psalter to hear personal words from the psalmists that reveal their attitudes and life experiences. David's sensitivities as one who was caught between the yes and no of faith, at least intellectually, are exposed in the magnificent poetry of Psalm 139. For an in-between moment, David launches out on a tangential journey through God's universe, exploring the potential highways and byways where he might sneak away from the view of his watchful God. But he discovers that God has claimed every nook and cranny of the universe; and he, the Creator God, is also the Redeemer God, pursuing those who contemplate an escape route from his presence. While David's contemplation sounds like he was looking for a getaway, his deliberation is more to the effect that there is no escape from the Creator of the universe and the Redeemer of humanity, even if one wanted to find such a path. David's life-passion is to be in the presence of the Lord (Ps. 23), and now, for whatever reason, he seems trapped between this passion and a fugitive mindset—or at least an intellectual path in the opposite direction: "Where shall I go from your Spirit? Or where shall I flee from your presence?" (139:7). This may be a rhetorical question, and if so, the answer is, Nowhere! The Creator God is the rudimentary thought of the poem, and David confesses that the Lord had created him in his mother's womb (139:13–16). More than that, his knowledge of the extremities of the universe to which he might flee is fixed in his mind, at least theoretically. Even the primordial darkness is a prospect for his hiding place, while he knows in truth that the hovering darkness has already been vanquished by the Creator-Redeemer's light: "Even the darkness is not dark to you; the night is bright as the day, for darkness is as light with you" (v. 12; see John 1:3–4). The Creator-Redeemer, despite the double-mindedness of the psalmist, or his theoretical plan, cannot dismiss this suppliant from his thoughts—the sum of his thoughts are astronomical!—and now David acknowledges that these thoughts were factored into his troubled life. This truth is the equivalent of Isaiah's covenant metaphor that also elicits the tender strains of a mother's love in Yahweh's covenant with Israel:

> Can a mother forget the baby at her breast
>   and have no compassion on the child she has borne?
> Though she may forget,
>   I will not forget you!

> See, I have engraved you on the palms of my hands;
> your walls are ever before me. (Isa. 49:15–16 NIV)

David reminds us of his awareness that God has hemmed him in on both sides (Ps. 139:5; see also Isa. 52:12), and his disposition is one of surrender, knowing that only God's search of his heart will reveal the "grievous way" whose removal will lead him to "the way everlasting" (Ps. 139:23–24).

The Creator-Redeemer God (Pss. 147 and 148)

In the larger context of Psalms 147 and 148, Psalm 147 is about the Creator God who is also the Redeemer God. While not diminishing the Creator's delight in his entire creation, our psalmist stresses God's delight in "those who fear him, in those who hope in his steadfast love" (*hesed*; v. 11). That is the suppliant's way of equating God and love, or coming close to doing so, a theological equation that John expresses so beautifully: "Anyone who does not love does not know God, because God is love" (1 John 4:8). The Redeemer God who "heals the brokenhearted, and binds up their wounds" (Ps. 147:3) is the Creator God whose intimacy with his creation also has a touching gentleness: "He determines the number of the stars; he gives to all of them their names" (v. 4). Charles Spurgeon captures the beauty of this verse in his own charming way: "The God of Israel is set forth in his peculiarity of glory as caring for the sorrowing, the insignificant, and forgotten. The poet finds a singular joy in extolling one who is so singularly gracious."[8] Crowning all of God's gracious deeds is the gift of his word, unique, intimate, and redeeming; "His word runs swiftly" (v. 15):

> He declares his word to Jacob,
> his statutes and rules to Israel.
> He has not dealt thus with any other nation;
> they do not know his rules.
> Praise the LORD. (Ps. 147:19–20)

Psalm 148 praises the Creator God, complementing the profile of the Redeemer God in Psalm 147, who is one and the same. This psalm of praise issues a call to the universe to praise the Lord: the angels; the created order, both animate and inanimate; kings and peoples of the earth, young and old

---

8. Spurgeon, *Treasury of David*, 3:414.

and children; and God's people, Israel. Beginning with the angels and the created order (vv. 1–6), the earth and its inhabitants acquire heaven's perfect pitch as they declare "his name alone is exalted" (vv. 7–14). Spiritually speaking, our psalmist has risen to that pinnacle of faith to which the Lord Jesus instructed us to aspire, when God's will is done "on earth as it is in heaven," and that includes perfect praise (Matt. 6:10).

The Superlative Praise of the Creator-Redeemer God (Ps. 150)

We have noted that Book 5 of the Psalter takes shape against the background of the return from the Babylonian exile and the rebuilding of the temple. In addition, we have also observed that David's passion was to be in the presence of the Lord, and that was the power that drove his temple-building aspirations. Psalm 150, the final psalm of the Psalter, locates the center of the praise of God "in his sanctuary" (*qodesh*) and implies that God's sanctuary is equivalent to the heavenly sanctuary of his creation (v. 1, "mighty heavens"; lit., "the firmament [*raqia*'] of his strength"; compare 19:1, "The firmament sheweth his handiwork" [KJV], and Gen. 1:6–8). We should also mention that no heavenly beings or nonhuman members of the created order are participants in this chorus as they are in Psalm 148:1–6, only the human family, the crown of God's creation and the object of his redeeming love. The earthly sanctuary (*qodesh*) and the heavenly sanctuary (firmament [*raqia*']) merge into the universal sanctuary that is filled with praise. The praise that fills the sanctuary is based on God's "mighty deeds" (*geburot*), referencing Yahweh's great redeeming acts in history, and God's "greatness" (*godel*), a summary term for God's attributes. The arc of God's character stretches across his great redeeming works to his exquisite character of "excellent greatness" (150:2), affirming the truth that creation and redemption are expressions of God's nature, sometimes given in terms of his love, sometimes in terms of his greatness, sometimes with other attributes; and there is no discrepancy between his acts and his being.

Erich Zenger's perceptive comments on Psalm 150 open up a vista that is particularly appropriate to our understanding of the psalm and its concluding position in the Psalter. Zenger detects a code language in the instrumental accompanists to the praise of God that leads us through the history of Israel's redemption and provides a template for our own chronicle of grace. The "trumpet sound" in verse 3a (shofar) in historical perspective announces the coronation of Israel's real King (2 Sam. 15:10; 1 Kings 1:34; 2 Kings 9:13; also Pss. 45:1; 149:2); the "lute and harp" of verse 3b celebrate the glory of the Lord that filled the temple upon its dedication (2 Chron 5:12–14); the "tambourine and dance" of verse 4a is an allusion to Yahweh's entry into the temple (Ps. 149:3); the "strings and pipe" of verse 4b allude to a great victory festival (Pss. 23:5; 96:9; 114:7); the "cymbals" of verse 5 suggest the prophetic day of the Lord (Zeph. 1:16); and the final call of verse 6 to "everything that has breath" (Gen. 2:7) is a summons to all humanity to praise the Lord.[9] Whatever pianissimos we encountered in Book 5, posed by Israel's exile and humiliation and other lamentations of humanity's fallen condition, now become not a fermata of adoration but an eternal crescendo of acclamation for all humanity to praise the Lord. It is a reminder of John's beautiful image of humankind's redemption as the 144,000, who have Christ's and the Father's names written on their foreheads, sing a "new song" that no one else can learn except those who have been redeemed from the earth (Rev. 14:3). Praise the Lord!

Other Biblical Warrants

The six-days-plus-seventh-day pattern of creation sets the two wonders of God's work of creation and redemption in relationship. When we read the creation narrative, we have to be especially sensitive to the subtle meanings of terms and expressions that to us may seem a little elusive, but to the ancient writers, and most likely their astute readers, were rhetorical jewels. Those writers were artists in their own world, and it is our duty as interpreters to enter their rhetorical world and admire their artistry so that we can better understand their message. That is indeed the case with the creation account as the master artist puts the finishing touch on the story: "And on the seventh day God finished his work that he had done, and he rested on the seventh day from all his work that he had done. So God blessed the seventh day and made it holy, because on it God rested from all his work that he had done in creation" (Gen. 2:2–3).

God's rest is a different category from his work, and even if our yet-unrefined understanding of this statement leaves its meaning a little murky, we have help from other biblical texts. For example, when Moses goes up Mount Sinai with Joshua and the elders, we are informed, "For six days the cloud covered the mountain, and on the seventh day the LORD called to Moses from within the cloud" (Exod. 24:16 NIV). The number pattern quite obviously hints at

9. Hossfeld and Zenger, *Psalms 3*, 659–60.

the six-days-plus-seventh-day pattern of creation. The reader should recall that the seventh day is the beginning of the age of redemption, just as Moses waits for Yahweh's revelation of the redeeming torah on the seventh day.

The writer to the Hebrews draws out that significance when he proclaims the Sabbath rest for the people of God—that is, the era of Christ's redeeming love. In fact, the author of Hebrews puts Psalm 95 and Genesis 2:2–3 in a rhetorical exchange. The Genesis text establishes the Sabbath rest for the people of God, and since there is no conclusion to the seventh day as there was to the first six days ("And there was evening and there was morning . . ."), the author of Hebrews takes that to mean that the seventh day was open-ended and still ongoing, and God's people, just as God had done, could enter the Sabbath rest through the sacrificial death of Christ.

Yet the author of Hebrews hears God's voice in Psalm 95 giving an update on how God's people had underperformed in redemptive history. In the psalmist's words to the disobedient first-generation Israelites who had come out of Egypt, the writer to the Hebrews hears the continuing openness of the Sabbath rest in the word "today" of Psalm 95:7: "Today, if you hear his voice, do not harden your hearts, as at Meribah, as on the day at Massah in the wilderness, when your fathers put me to the test. . . . Therefore I swore in my wrath, 'They shall not enter my rest'" (Ps. 95:7–9, 11). The author of Hebrews sees the entrance to Canaan as the fulfillment of the Sabbath rest by God's people, but the first generation of the exodus did not enter, so the Sabbath rest was still open—"Today" (Heb. 3:1–4:13). Yet by God's design, the true Sabbath rest was the redemption that Christ had accomplished on the cross, and that was the Sabbath rest that the author admonishes his readers to "strive to enter" so that no one perishes by following the example of the first post-exodus generation (Heb. 4:11). Moreover, it is probably not coincidental that Psalm 95 weaves together strains of creation (95:3–5) and redemption (95:6–11).

As interpreters of Scripture, we should recall that the Old Testament writers laid down the template on which the final and conclusive spiritual realities of redeeming grace are placed. It should not therefore escape our notice that when John writes the final chapter of redemption, he tells the story of "a new heaven and a new earth" (Rev. 21:1). It is the story of redemption voiced in the language of creation: "And he who was seated on the throne said, 'Behold, I am making all things new'" (21:5).[10]

10. Bullock, *Psalms*, 2:242–43.

TWO

Hesed, God's Steadfast Love

The Boundless Measure of God's Love

In our effort to understand God's profile as we see it in the Psalms, there is no topic more important than God's love. The Hebrew word *hesed,* more than any other word in the Hebrew Bible and much like the Greek word *agapē* in the New Testament, is the key to understanding the character of God. It appears 245 times in the Old Testament, 127 of those in the book of Psalms. While word counts are not necessarily an accurate index into biblical theology, this particular count is a good indicator of the importance of the word *hesed.* Its English rendering, from the time of Myles Coverdale's translation of the Bible (AD 1535) and onward in the English Bible tradition, was generally associated with God's love. Coverdale's translation as "loving-kindness" and "mercy" was pretty much followed by the Geneva Bible of 1560. The King James Version of 1611, heir to the popularity of the Geneva translation, generally rendered *hesed* as "steadfast love" and "lovingkindness," continuing the connection to God's love. The nuance of "steadfast love" intimates the unchanging nature of God's love. The Revised Standard Version (1952), which follows the legacy of the King James Version, preserved that translation tradition, and the popular New International Version (New Testament, 1973; Old Testament and New Testament, 1978) generally rendered the word as "love" or "unfailing love." In a slightly different sense, it could be rendered God's "unrelenting love" because it captures a nuance that is so beautifully depicted in Psalms 106 and 107 in an alternating cycle between rebellion/distress and God's deliverance (see table 1).

Table 1. Rebellion/Distress and Deliverance in Psalms 106 and 107

Psalm 106		Psalm 107	
Rebellion/distress	Deliverance	Rebellion/distress	Deliverance
106:6–7	106:8–12	107:4–5	107:6–9
106:13–22	106:23	107:10–12	107:13–16
106:24–29	106:30–31	107:17–18	107:19–22
106:34–42	106:44–46	107:23–27	107:28–32

While the different translations—steadfast love, unfailing love, mercy, goodness, loving-kindness, unrelenting love, and love—provide slightly different nuances on *hesed*, it is still impossible, despite the plurality of expression, to measure the "love" of God in the Psalms. Yet the psalmists make a great effort to do just that by use of metaphors, since that was the best way to say God's love was boundless and unchanging. The terms of the text are intended to leave the reader in awe and wonder, and Psalm 103 introduces three metaphors to accomplish that.

The first metaphor is the reference to the height of the heavens above the earth to describe the limitlessness of God's love: "For as high as the heavens are above the earth, so great is his steadfast love toward those who fear him" (Ps. 103:11)—that's the vertical dimension. The ancients were in wonder about the extent of the heavens, and modern science has magnified our knowledge of the boundless dimensions of the universe and for all practical purposes has augmented the wonder. The other two metaphors describe the horizontal dimension of God's love, or how it operates within human society.

The second of the three metaphors for God's love in Psalm 103 is the measurement of the distance between the east and the west, a measure of God's forgiveness that flows out of his love: "As far as the east is from the west, so far does he remove our transgressions from us" (Ps. 103:12). The ancient Israelites did not think in terms of a round world but envisioned one that could, in the imagination at least, be measured from one end to the other. Still, contained in the bounds of the metaphor is a measureless quantity of love.

The third metaphor is drawn from the intimacy of family life, tapping into the image of earthly fathers and their children: "As a father shows compassion to his children, so the Lord shows compassion to those who fear him" (Ps. 103:13). All parents who love their children know the meaning of this metaphor, although the heavenly Father's compassion exceeds even that of human fathers. Further, to put God's love in historical context, David quotes from the second Sinai covenant (Exod. 34:6), a covenant that followed upon Israel's sin with the golden calf (Exod. 32). Called the formula of grace (Exod. 34:6–7), this covenantal promise that the Lord makes to Israel is alluded to numerous times in the Psalter and quoted three times (Pss. 86:15; 103:8; 145:8).

Nelson Glueck in his seminal study of *hesed* identified the term as covenantal,[1] and the covenantal value of the term, however it is translated, is monumentally significant. It is thus no surprise that the Psalter is replete with terms and descriptions of the second Sinai covenant. Nor is it of small consequence that the formula of grace follows Israel's primal engagement with idolatry, the sin that ultimately would lead them into exile and threaten their existence.

The psalmic portrait of the world controlled by love (*hesed*) generally meets us in the Psalms in brief snatches, which—instead of diminishing the message—has the effect, by its pervasive presence, of magnifying it. That is to say that God's love is so important that it is written into the structure of the Psalter. More often than not, the portrait of the world, righted with love, is pitted against a portrait of the world degraded by evil.

Psalm 36 is an example of a psalm that provides the double portrait of evil and love over against each other. Psalm 36:1–4 paints a picture of this world where there is "no fear of God before their eyes" (v. 1 NIV), evidenced by self-flattery, deceitful talk, and unrelenting malicious plots against fellow human beings. Then our word artist turns to the other portrait that counterbalances, even countermands, the first and evokes a multiplex of divine virtues: "Your *steadfast love,* O LORD, extends to the heavens, your *faithfulness* to the clouds. Your *righteousness* is like the mountains of God [NIV: "highest mountains"]; your *judgments* are like the great deep; man and beast you save, O LORD" (vv. 5–6). Both "love" (*hesed*) and "faithfulness" (*'emunah*)[2] occur in the formula of grace (Exod. 34:6), and in Psalm 36:5 they occur as parallel terms, most likely, as Glueck suggests, functioning as a hendiadys,[3] meaning "faithful love" or "covenant love." The two terms that follow, "righteousness" (*tsidqah*) and "judgment" (*mishpat*) are the products of God's faithful love

---

1. Glueck, *Ḥesed in the Bible,* 54–55.
2. *'emunah* ("faithfulness") is often used as a synonym of *'emet* ("faithfulness/truth"), the latter being the term that occurs in Exod. 34:6.
3. Glueck, *Ḥesed in the Bible,* 79. A hendiadys is composed of two words, connected by "and," that convey a single idea. The second word functions as a modifier, in this case "faithfulness" (a noun) functions adjectivally, "faithful."

as it is put into effect in the world of human affairs. The psalmist is obviously speaking from his earthly perspective as he describes divine love that operates in the world with its dimensions so boundless that it "extends to the heavens, your [Yahweh's] faithfulness to the clouds" (v. 5). While we may think this description of God's love comes up slightly shy of ubiquity, the psalmist reaches to the outer limits of his language to say God's love is everywhere and countermands the evils of this world. It reminds us of John's assertion that "he who is in you is greater than he who is in the world" (1 John 4:4).

God's Love, the Shaper and Victor of History

God's love is the only power that can conquer and vanquish evil's forces in the world, and in Psalm 36:12 we have a picture of the battlefield littered with casualties: "There the evildoers lie fallen; they are thrust down, unable to rise." Love has triumphed! "How precious is your steadfast love, O God!" (v. 7). This means, on the horizontal level of human life, that righteousness and justice have prevailed. Love and faithfulness belong among God's shared attributes. And most importantly, to please the Lord, we humans must practice love and faithfulness and reflect God's character in the world he created and redeemed.

Psalm 103 is essentially a minor treatise on the formula of grace, quoting it in verse 8: "The LORD is merciful and gracious, slow to anger and abounding in steadfast love." As we saw in our review of Psalm 103 above, David reiterates the boundless measure of God's love (*hesed*), stressing four divine attributes, God's (1) love, (2) forgiveness, (3) compassion, and (4) anger (Exod. 34:6–7).

Drawing metaleptically[4] on the context of the formula of grace (Exod. 34:6–7)—the idolatrous incident of the golden calf—David pronounces the formula to be the Lord's admission that his love is primary, for "he does not deal with us according to our sins" (Ps. 103:10). Among all of Israel's sins—and ours—idolatry is the lowest depth of sin because it essentially eliminates God and puts the human creature in God's place.[5] But despite the self-deifying sin of idolatry, God's love intercepts his judgment and repays us according

4. Richard Hays defines "metalepsis" as "a rhetorical and poetic device in which one text alludes to an earlier text in a way that evokes resonances of the earlier text beyond those explicitly cited. The result is that the interpretation of a metalepsis requires the reader to recover unstated or suppressed correspondences between the two texts." Hays, *Echoes of Scripture in the Letters of Paul*, 2.
5. See "Original Sin as Idolatry: Genesis 3" in chap. 9.

to God's love, not according to our sins, even the grossest of them. It is a colossal exchange!

God's love is also one of his shared attributes, which means that God shares his love with humankind and commands them to share it with their fellow human beings. God's love, a most desirable trait for humans to emulate, channeled in and through the human creatures, characterizes those who fear him (Ps. 36:10) and who keep his commandments (119:149, 159). The crowning object of Israel's life—and ours—is the worship of our immortal God. Psalm 48:9 puts that in the context of temple worship: "We have thought on your steadfast love [*hesed*], O God, in the midst of your temple." God's love, the magnetic mystery that brings life and worship together, leaves our notion of the secular and sacred in shambles. The prophet Micah understood this power of *hesed* and summed it up in his unforgettable oracle: "He has told you, O man, what is good; and what does the LORD require of you but to do justice, and to love kindness [*hesed*], and to walk humbly with your God?" (Mic. 6:8). The gist of the prophet's admonition is that practicing justice and loving-kindness/mercy (*hesed*) are the required curriculum for walking humbly with God. (See chap. 15, "Finding God in the Fabric of the World.")

We have already seen the particularity of the word *hesed* and the expansive notion it represents. At the same time, we might be correctly warned that the occurrence of the word in Psalm 107:1 ("for his steadfast love [*hesed*] endures forever") might not capture the fullness of the covenantal commitment to which the Scriptures attest. The survival and triumph of the Hebrew faith in the ancient world constitute a complex story that is not explained merely by the theological uniqueness of Judaism and the wide-ranging success and spread of Christianity, though those stories are thrillers. Yet we can be sure that those success stories are deeply embedded in the story of God's unfailing love, for it was unique in the ancient world, and the sequel to the story as we have it in the New Testament would never have been written without the centrality of God's love in the Hebrew Bible, especially in the Psalms. It is doubtful that John could ever have written the unadorned declaration "God is love" (1 John 4:8) had there been no Hebrew Scriptures. The New Testament is not as "new" as we might sometimes assume. It is built on the foundation of the Old Testament and the portrait of God that is encoded there.

The concentration of God's *hesed* in the Psalms is no accident because the Psalms are an anthology of Israel's prayers and meditations through the centuries. We would expect a theological truth so important as God's love to find frequent occurrence. As we have already observed, God's love is a many-sided truth, and every time we turn it, a new aspect—not a new truth—is likely to appear. So we should look for the sparkle that this slight movement produces, especially in its power to shape individual believers and the community of faith. David had a sense of this shaping experience, one that was not always delightful but needful, and he says, "Surely goodness and love [hesed] shall pursue [rdp] me all the days of my life" (Ps. 23:6 AT). God's goodness and love were David's "shepherd dogs," as some Scottish preachers are fond of saying, to lead David (Ps. 23:3–4), and when necessary to drive him into the house of the Lord. Beyond that, we would suppose that the thought of building the temple was never far from David's mind, and Psalm 23:6 is an allusion to David's passion for the temple, as he recognized the part that God's pursuing love played in the temple aspect of his life and reign.

One of the most moving aspects of hesed in the Psalms, and at the same time one of the least recognized, is the force of God's love as the mover of history. This feature is especially built into the use of this term in Book 5 (Pss. 107–50), which opens with the declarative force of this term in Psalm 107:1: "Give thanks to the LORD, for he is good, for his love [hesed] endures forever" (AT). The theme of love punctuates the entire psalm in the second of two refrains of each strophe, as the psalmist follows a well-structured outline in his review of four scenarios of life and demonstrates how Yahweh responds when his erring people call upon him for help. The cycle is much like that of the book of Judges:

- God's people are troubled by formidable forces
- First refrain—a cry to the Lord for help
- The Lord's deliverance
- Second refrain—a call to give thanks for the Lord's hesed
- God's acts of steadfast love

We should note that the Lord's love appears consistently in the second refrain: "Let them thank the LORD for his steadfast love [hesed], for his wonderful works to the children of man!" (Ps. 107:8). Then follows the Hebrew word "for" (ki), which carries a causal meaning ("because"), and the psalmist fills in the blessings that come to God's people as a result of his love. God's love and the events of history are in a causal relationship.

Psalm 136, a psalm that functions as a literary and theological crown on the Psalms of Ascent (Pss. 120–34),[6] provides a clearer example of the love of God as the force that moves the historical process. The psalm celebrates God's love as the undergirding and energizing power of creation and redemption, employing the refrain "for/because his steadfast love [*hesed*] endures forever" (AT) twenty-six times in the psalm. So forceful is that one word that we can say God's reason for creating the world was love, and his reason for redeeming the world was love. The key that unlocks all of God's good gifts is love.

God's love (*hesed*) reveals the true nature of the divine, and the mysteries of his love are "marvelous in our eyes." Psalm 118 entertains the mystery of the stone the builders rejected, and glories in the marvel that the rejected stone had become the cornerstone of the new temple. Who would ever think that God would manifest his love in the weak, the poor and needy, the despised and rejected, and dwell in an earthly, human-made temple! Further, when we observe that Psalm 118 begins with a fourfold announcement that God's *hesed* endures forever (vv. 1–4) and concludes with the same declaration (v. 29), we should recognize that the rejected stone was a dynamic function of God's love, which engages the rejected and weak and transforms them into the triumph of his will: "This is the LORD's doing; it is marvelous in our eyes" (v. 23). When history moves under the momentum of God's love, we can better accept its twists and turns and rejoice in the story of God's steadfast love. The Lord Jesus himself quoted Psalm 118:22–23 to say that he was "the stone that the builders rejected" (Mark 12:10–11), and it is not an overstatement to say that his humility and suffering for the world's redemption, energized by *agapē* love, turned the world upside down, which was in effect the world turned right side up.

God's Love in the Meet-and-Greet Moment of God's Eternal Kingdom

The Psalms are a treasure trove of spiritual metaphors, and often we read them so quickly and unpretentiously that we miss their power. The Revelation of John is another masterful resource for metaphors. One is the marriage supper of the Lamb in Revelation 19:9: "And the angel said to me, 'Write this: Blessed

---

6. Psalm 135 crowns the Songs of Ascent (Pss. 120–34) with its rejection of idolatry as the theological centerpiece of the biblical faith, and Ps. 136 is the crown of crowns that proclaims Yahweh's steadfast love (*hesed*) as the true operating principle of the faith.

are those who are invited to the marriage supper of the Lamb.' And he said to me, 'These are the true words of God.'" While some interpreters will insist that this should be taken literally—and that's my hope too—the important truth is what the metaphor means. This is John's way of describing the final moment of redemption when Christ the Groom and his church the Bride are united in the world's most blessed union, the nuptial of all nuptials, the eschatological day when God's redeeming love has fulfilled his eternal purpose. Whatever the details of the celebration, John thought marriage not a strange metaphor for God and redeemed humanity (see Hosea) but the appropriate metaphor for this inimitable moment.

Psalm 85:10 also introduces such a metaphor, slightly short of the metaphor of a wedding but still in keeping with the ideas of love and faithfulness: "Steadfast love and faithfulness meet; righteousness and peace kiss each other." These divine attributes, certainly never strangers (cf. Ps. 89:14) and sealed in the vows of covenant (Exod. 34:6), are God's emissaries of salvation in this meet-and-greet moment of redemption. Metaphorically speaking, it is the moment when God's steadfast love delivers its inestimable gift of grace to the people of God. Righteousness, generally captioned in terms of social justice (Deut. 16:18–20), and peace, which is the resulting gift of reigning righteousness, describe a world made vertically right with God and horizontally right with one another. The Psalms and prophetic books have a penchant for describing this eschatological moment. Derek Kidner calls this metaphor "one of the most satisfying descriptions of concord—spiritual, moral and material—to be found anywhere in Scripture."[7] In contrast to the kiss of Psalm 2:12 ("kiss the Son"), which is the humiliating kiss of surrender to the conqueror, this is the kiss of love. If there is any shadow of conquest around this metaphor, it is the conquest of love, and how indescribably precious is that reality!

7. Kidner, *Psalms 73–150*, 308.

THREE

Thinking Comprehensively about God's Goodness (*Tob*)

God's Goodness Inherent in Creation

Having discussed the nature of God's love (*hesed*) in chapter 2, it is appropriate for us to consider briefly God's goodness (*tob*), the wider theological environment in which God's love functions. In fact, it is a concept that the opening chapter of Genesis lays before us. As we read that chapter, it is one of those terms that are so obvious and yet so easily passed over in order to give other terms in the narrative their due. When the master plan of Scripture begins to come in view, piece by piece like a jigsaw puzzle, we begin to understand better the Mastermind behind the master plan. It can be argued, of course, that such associations can be overvalued, but they can also be undervalued, and perhaps God's goodness is one of those terms that suffers the latter offense more severely than the former. Obviously, we have to look for literary signs and theological associations, and in connection to God's goodness we find them in Genesis. Six times in the creation narrative of Genesis 1, God's creation receives the divine stamp of approval with the statement "and God saw that it was good," implying that the Creator who made it was good (vv. 4, 10, 12, 18, 21, 25). In the seventh occurrence of God's approval, all creation is made the subject of the sentence: "God saw everything that he had made, and behold, *it was very good*" (v. 31). The fact that God recognizes the goodness of creation is a reflection of his character, and the number seven, being the perfect number, may also hint that the perfect Creator had called into existence the perfect creation. Thus, the goodness of the created world and by implication the goodness of God are established before the initial story of creation's ruin is recorded in Genesis 3.

God's Goodness Inherent in the Covenant

Another piece of the master plan falls into place after the golden calf debacle of Exodus 32–34. Instead of leading to God's abandonment and destruction of his people, which Israel might have expected, it leads to the second Sinai covenant, recorded in Exodus 34:6–7, already discussed in some detail above. In a rather surprising and puzzling announcement, the Lord tells Moses he will not go with the Israelites into Canaan because of their idolatry at Mount Horeb, lest "I consume you on the way" (Exod. 33:3). The deity's indecisiveness is not merely an anthropopathic touch. Rather it, along with many other descriptive pieces of information in Scripture about God, reveals something about his remarkable nature: God can contemplate alternatives, which is an aspect of his freedom, even alternatives that contradict his character, but he can act only according to his nature: "He does all that he pleases" (Ps. 115:3). That means God's acts are a function of his character, making God's works a key to his profile. This is one major reason the Psalms invite us to observe the Lord's works: through them we learn who he is.

The exchange between the Lord and Moses ends with the Lord's "change of mind" to go with the Israelites into Canaan after all, and further, to do anything Moses asks of the Lord. In response Moses makes his request, "Please show me your glory" (Exod. 33:18), whereupon the Lord offers to make his "goodness" pass before Moses, because seeing the Lord's glory was virtually the same as seeing his face, and no one could see God's face and live (vv. 12–23): "I will make all my goodness pass before you, and I will proclaim before you my name, 'the LORD'" (v. 19). Then when Moses had prepared two new tablets, we are informed that "the LORD descended in the cloud and stood with him there, and proclaimed the name of the LORD. The LORD passed before him and proclaimed, 'The LORD, the LORD, a God merciful and gracious, slow to anger, and abounding in steadfast love and faithfulness, keeping steadfast love for thousands, forgiving iniquity and transgression and sin, but who will by no means clear the guilty, visiting the iniquity of the fathers on the children and the children's children, to the third and the fourth generation"

(34:5–7). Although the Lord's "goodness" *(tob)* is not described as such, the text makes it clear that the Lord's name and his goodness are synonymous. There is no better description of God in the Old Testament than here, and this is the God who will go with Israel into Canaan—a remarkable profile, especially when held up against Israel's stiff-necked ("stubborn") disposition.

The Psalms quote and allude to other Hebrew Scriptures,[1] and all who are interested in how Scripture has been interpreted through the centuries should give thanks for this gift; it is an ancient chapter in the history of biblical interpretation, indeed a chapter on how Scripture interprets Scripture. Psalm 86 is an excellent example of this phenomenon, quoting Exodus 34:6, and when we look at the psalm as a whole, we see that David does more than quote Exodus; he actually incorporates its vocabulary in the psalm.[2] That feature gives the impression that the golden calf episode and the covenant renewal that followed were in David's mind as he wrote.

God's Goodness Inherent in the Kingdom

As Psalm 135 follows the Songs of Ascent (Pss. 120–34) with its power and beauty, the psalmist declares that God's goodness is reason to praise the Lord: "Praise the LORD, *for the LORD is good;* sing to his name, for it is pleasant!" (135:3). This reminds us of the equivalence we have identified in Exodus 34 between the Lord's name and his goodness. Once the psalmist has issued this reminder, he rehearses God's deeds in Israel's history, which are expressions of God's goodness (135:4–12).

The notion of God's kingdom is strong in the Prophets and Psalms. It is not a geographical realm, although that is not necessarily excluded, but it is a spiritual order, shaped by God's righteousness and imputed with the abundance of God's goodness. To put it another way, it is the story of God's redeeming work in history, both Israel's and the world's. Psalm 145, the final David psalm in the Psalter, turns its attention to the kingdom of God, referring to it twice as "your [Yahweh's] kingdom" (145:11, 13). Significantly, David again quotes Exodus 34:6: "The LORD is gracious and merciful, slow to anger

---

1. See "Reflecting on Methodology" in "Introductory Matters."

2. "Gracious" (Ps. 86:3, 15, 16 [*hnn*]); "compassionate" (86:15 [*rhm*]); "abounding in steadfast love" (86:5 [*rab hesed*]); "abounding in steadfast love and faithfulness" (86:15 [*rab hesed we'emet*]); "truth" (86:11 [*'emet*]); "steadfast love" (86:13 [*hesed*]); "slow to anger" (86:15 [*'erek 'appayim*]).

and abounding in steadfast love" (145:8); and in the next verse David lauds the Lord who "is good to all, and his mercy is over all that he has made," combining God's compassion and goodness as the operating principle of God's kingdom. The goodness of God opens Yahweh's profile to us.

And just as importantly, David's title as "servant" has preempted his title as "king," the latter now reserved for God: "I will extol you, my God and King" (145:1). Even though the noun "kingdom" occurs in the psalm, the poem is really about the King, not the kingdom. In ancient Near Eastern societies, absolute kingship was the rule—the king *was* the kingdom—and that notion is conferred on Yahweh. Why would we not want an absolute King who is "gracious and merciful, slow to anger and abounding in steadfast love"! The fact that David is never called king in this final David collection of psalms (Pss. 138–45) is not coincidental. If we advance a thousand years from David, we hear the voice of another humble servant articulating David's message: "He must increase, but I must decrease" (John 3:30).

FOUR

Yahweh's Condescension in the Psalter

The Multiportraiture of Yahweh in the Psalter

The Psalter, being a repository of Israel's theology through the centuries, is filled with a broad range of descriptions, meditations, and testimonies about God's character. Most of us, when looking for a descriptor that captures the portrait of God we have in mind, hasten to the Psalms. From prosecuting attorney to defense witness (Ps. 109); from the exalted Lord who sits enthroned on high to the humbled Savior who "raises the poor from the dust," never compromising his sovereign reign (Ps. 113, v. 7); from Creator of a good world to Redeemer who forgives the sins of a fallen world (Ps. 65); from the architect and builder of Jerusalem to the healer of shattered hearts (Ps. 147). These descriptive titles are only a sampling of what we find in the Psalms.

Of the many portraits of Yahweh in the Psalter, two of them stand out at the heart of biblical theology, and at first glimpse, they seem to stand at opposite poles. They are the *exalted Yahweh* and the *humbled Yahweh*. Yet, when the heavenly God comes down to earth, especially when Yahweh self-identifies with his human creatures—which often in the Psalter are the poor and needy—this is not merely a metaphor but a theological statement about the divine nature: that condescension, God's self-manifestation in suffering and humility, is endemic to his nature. Even though the concept of divine condescension is more central to the Christian faith than to Judaism, the portrait is not lost on the Jewish faith. The Babylonian Talmud preserves a beautiful portrait of God in the words of first-century Rabbi Jochanan, who recognizes this divine likeness in all three portions of the Hebrew Bible:

> Wherever you find [mentioned in the Scriptures] the power of the Holy One, blessed be He, you also find his gentleness mentioned. This fact is stated in the Torah, repeated in the Prophets, and stated a third time in the [Sacred] Writings. It is written in the Torah, For the Lord your God, he is the God of gods and Lord of lords, and it says immediately afterwards, He doth execute justice for the fatherless and widow. It is repeated in the Prophets: For thus saith the High and Lofty One, that inhabiteth eternity, whose name is holy, and it says immediately afterwards, [I dwell] with him that is of a contrite and humble spirit. It is stated a third time in the [Sacred] Writings, as it is written: Extol him that rideth upon the skies, whose name is the Lord, and immediately afterwards it is written, A father of the fatherless and a judge of the widows.[1]

The doctrine of divine condescension is the expression of Yahweh's identity with humanity, and in that identity the poor and needy and oppressed find *their* identity and *their* salvation (e.g., Ps. 76:8–9). It is the embryonic expression of the doctrine of the incarnation. In fact, the Old Testament puts its signature on the incipient doctrine in signs and shadows, anticipating and awaiting the reality of God's assumption of human flesh in Jesus of Nazareth. As a consequence, when we encounter the doctrine of the incarnation in the New Testament, mysterious and marvelous, it may come as a joyful wonder but not as a total shock—we have the sense that we have seen a shadow of this doctrine before.

Moreover, while the incarnation of God in Christ brings together the exalted and humbled portraits of the divine and engages us in paradoxical thought, the opposites are not contradictory. G. K. Chesterton expresses the truth of this doctrine in his unique way: "Christianity is the only religion on earth that has felt that omnipotence made God incomplete."[2] John's prologue to his Gospel puts the doctrine in memorable form: "And the Word became flesh and dwelt among us, and we have seen his glory" (John 1:14).

1. Babylonian Talmud, Megillah 31a.
2. Chesterton, *Orthodoxy*, 17.

The Exalted Yahweh Credentialed by Creation and His Unique Reign

It is not at all difficult to identify the portrait of the exalted Yahweh in the Psalter—it is everywhere! While this portrait has many expressions, two of the most prominent are his creation of the world and his providential command of nature and human affairs. Psalm 104, a creation psalm, reminds us that Yahweh "set the earth on its foundations, so that it should never be moved" (v. 5), and he made the moon and sun, in addition to creating and maintaining both the animal kingdom and the human race. Yahweh is both Creator and Sustainer, and his relationship to the created world is so intimate and powerful that he covers himself with light as with a garment; "he makes the clouds his chariot; he rides on the wings of the wind; he makes his messengers winds, his ministers a flaming fire" (vv. 2–4). And in the next to the last David psalm of the Psalter, David prays passionately, "Bow your heavens, O Lord, and come down! . . . Stretch out your hand from on high; rescue me and deliver me from the many waters, from the hand of foreigners" (Ps. 144:5, 7). The idea is that when the Lord appears to help his people, he "comes down." It is not simply a movement; it is a theological statement.

In Book 5, Israel's king, whose preferred title now is the Lord's servant, prays the prayer that had lodged in his soul over the years of his reign—that Yahweh would deliver him from his enemies. As his vision widens from the earthly kingdom to the kingdom of God, especially in the last collection of David psalms (Pss. 138–45), David anchors his hope in the steadfast love of God, "gracious and merciful, slow to anger and abounding in steadfast love" (Ps. 145:8; Exod. 34:6). And in company with his servants who are "falling" and "bowed down," he says, "The Lord upholds all who are falling and raises up all who are bowed down" (Ps. 145:14). The picture is of Yahweh, standing on common ground with his people, lifting them up.

Among the strongest descriptions of Yahweh's exalted estate is the contrast with lifeless idols in Book 5, a symbol of Israel's rejection of idolatry. According to Ezekiel, idolatry was the reason for the exile in the first place (Ezek. 36:16–18; implied in Ezek. 14:11 and 37:23). As the nation faces the challenge of restoring temple worship, Book 5 raises the signal of victory and repeats this derisive confession of Yahweh's supremacy over idols in two places: in the middle of the Egyptian Hallel[3] (Ps. 115:4–8) and in the psalm that crowns the Songs of Ascent (135:15–18). The psalmist polemicizes against the nations'

---

3. The Egyptian Hallel is Pss. 113–18. See further below.

gods that are made of silver and gold, and out of their strident unbelief the nations ask, "Where is their [Israel's] God?" (115:2):

> Their idols are silver and gold,
>   the work of human hands.
> They have mouths, but do not speak;
>   eyes, but do not see.
> They have ears, but do not hear;
>   noses, but do not smell.
> They have hands, but do not feel;
>   feet, but do not walk;
>   and they do not make a sound in their throat. (Ps. 115:4–7)

The answer is an effective denial of the idols, who are lifeless—"The dead do not praise the LORD" (115:17); but far from being lifeless and idle, "Our God is in the heavens," which Yahweh also made (115:3). How could lifeless idols make the heavens! Thus Yahweh's credentials as sovereign ruler of the universe are that he is Creator of the world and he is the only living God in the universe.

Psalm 2 lowers our attention to the earthly sphere and gives witness to Yahweh's control over the world of humanity, especially the rulers of the earth who, in their power-bloated minds, think they can even overpower God. But the true Ruler of the world has a perspective that earthly rulers have difficulty comprehending, and Yahweh laughs at the deluded rulers who think they can gain ascendency over Yahweh (Ps. 2:4; see chap. 7, "The Laughter of God"). Then when the lesson of Yahweh's sovereign rule over the world of nature and humanity has been learned through the powerful testimony of the Psalms, the concluding collection of praises (Pss. 146–50) summons all creation to praise the Lord, who "builds up Jerusalem," "gathers the outcasts of Israel," "heals the broken hearted," "binds up their wounds," and "determines the number of the stars," even calls them by name (Ps. 147:2–5). In this final paean of praise, the two pictures of Yahweh come together, and we see him as the creating (exalted) and healing (humbled) God.

The Humbled Yahweh Who Condescends to Help His Earthly Creatures

That brings us to the second part of our portrait, the humbled Yahweh, who also inhabits earthly institutions and humbles himself to help the poor and needy and oppressed. This plan is called the covenant formula, as we have discussed above, and its outline and substance are already present in the Pentateuch. In fact, the trifold nature of this formula is laid out in Leviticus 26:11–12: "I will make my dwelling among you, . . . And I will walk among you and dwell among you and will be your God, and you shall be my people." It is not coincidental that the Lord's presence among his people is primary and the longest of the three parts as we have them in the Levitical formula. While this order is not always the same, it is significant that in the final chapter of the so-called Holiness Code (Lev. 17–26), addressed to the people of Israel, we have a relational code assuring Israel of Yahweh's presence, his condescension to dwell among them. Summarized as (1) I will be your God, (2) you shall be my people, and (3) I will dwell in your midst, it is the microcosmic view of biblical theology.

The idea that Yahweh promises to dwell among his people assumes a multifaceted form in the Psalter. Its most elevated form occurs as dwelling in God's presence or in the house of the Lord (e.g., Ps. 23:6), and even seeing the Lord's face (Ps. 17:15). While seeing God's face is the climactic experience, the Psalms reveal God to us in everyday life, including protection from danger, providential care in general, and the application of Yahweh's steadfast love (see chap. 15, "Finding God in the Fabric of the World"). As Psalm 113:4–9 attests, the exalted Yahweh, exalted above the heavens, condescends (v. 6; NIV "stoops" [*mashpil*]) and "raises the poor from the dust and lifts the needy from the ash heap, to make them sit with princes of his people. He gives the barren woman a home, making her the joyous mother of children" (vv. 7–9).

The portrait of the humbled Yahweh is connected to the Genesis story of God's primordial grief regarding humanity's sin: "And the LORD was sorry that he had made humankind on the earth, and it grieved [*'tsb*] him to his heart" (Gen. 6:6 NRSV). Sadly, God's sorrow even turned in the direction of obliterating his creation. But if we watch the biblical narrative carefully, we will note that God's sorrow turns ultimately in the direction of positive action, as in the Genesis story when "Noah found grace in the eyes of the LORD" (Gen. 6:8 KJV). It is the paradigm of divine sorrow answered by divine grace that we see in many other portions of Scripture. The sorrow of God and the response of grace took the form of the covenant in the Noah story when Yahweh codified the rebellious nature of humankind and divine mercy: "Then Noah built an altar to the LORD and took some of every clean animal and some of every clean bird and offered burnt offerings on the altar. And when the LORD smelled the pleasing aroma, the LORD said in his heart, 'I will never again curse the ground because of man, for the intention of man's heart is evil from his youth. Neither will I ever again strike down every living creature as I have done. While the earth remains, seedtime and harvest, cold and heat, summer and winter, day and night, shall not cease'" (Gen. 8:20–22).

The Abrahamic covenant followed the covenant with Noah (Gen. 12:1–3), incarnating it in one man and his offspring, Israel, "a kingdom of priests and a holy nation" (Exod. 19:5–6). Then came the second Sinai covenant, formulated as a response to the brazen idolatrous golden calf debacle at Sinai (Exod. 34:6–7). This covenant, the formula of grace, cited in many instances in this theology, is alluded to numerous times in the Psalter and installed as strategic guideposts at three points in the Psalms: 86:15 (Book 3); 103:8 (Book 4); 145:8 (Book 5).[4] When Israel had committed the most detestable sin at Sinai, God reaffirmed his gracious love for them and, we should add, for all of us: "The LORD, the LORD, a God merciful and gracious, slow to anger, and abounding in steadfast love and faithfulness," concluding with the promise of Yahweh's forgiveness (Exod. 34:6–7).

As a magnificent illustration of Yahweh's love, when Israel had been caught up in pagan worship, the prophet Hosea cast their relationship to God in terms of a father and his beloved infant. The Lord could not forget those tender days when he taught Israel to walk and took him up in his arms:

> When Israel was a child, I loved him,
>   and out of Egypt I called my son.
> The more they were called,
>   the more they went away;
> they kept sacrificing to the Baals,
>   and burning offerings to idols.
>
> Yet it was I who taught Ephraim to walk;
>   I took them up by their arms,
>   but they did not know that I healed them.
> I led them with cords of kindness,
>   with the bands of love,
> and I came to them as one who eases the yoke on their jaws,
>   and I bent down to them and fed them. (Hosea 11:1–4)

4. See the discussion in Bullock, "Covenant Renewal and the Formula of Grace," 18–34.

However, despite the idolatrous response Israel made to Yahweh's fatherly love, Yahweh acted out of his compassion, having registered his love and compassion formally in the covenant relationship, even though his thoughts turned again toward abandonment and destruction. Yet, like a loving parent with a wayward child, Yahweh's unfailing and unrequited love overwhelmed every thought of abandonment. The prophet's description of Yahweh's compassion is one of the most touching moments in the redemption story as Yahweh agonizingly soliloquizes over the matter and reaches a resolution of grace:

> How can I give you up, O Ephraim?
>> How can I hand you over, O Israel?
> How can I make you like Admah?
>> How can I treat you like Zeboiim?
> My heart recoils within me;
>> my compassion grows warm and tender.
> I will not execute my burning anger;
>> I will not again destroy Ephraim;
> for I am God and not a man,
>> the Holy One in your midst,
>> and I will not come in wrath. (Hosea 11:8–9)

In two other instances in the Old Testament the verb "grieve" (*'tsb*) is used of God's inner mourning (Ps. 78:40; Isa. 63:10). God's grief implies an intimacy with his creation, an intimacy that naturally exists because God had created humankind in his image, and that relationship forever connected God and humanity—it could not be broken. When we hear Yahweh's promise in the covenant formula, "I will dwell in your midst," human sin and rebellion against God join in the antiphonal liturgy of grace and echo in the chambers of the world where that human/divine dwelling takes place, where the humbled God meets sinful humanity in its lost estate.

These observations help us understand Peter's declaration that God provided for our redemption through the precious blood of Christ "before the foundation of the world" (1 Pet. 1:19–20; also Rev. 13:8; 17:8). That means that God's eternal plan made provision for our redemption, and God's creation of humanity in his image is a hint of that truth. Even though the phrase "image of God" never occurs in the Old Testament after Genesis 9:6, the Psalter is an echo chamber for the story of redemption, most often echoing Yahweh's redeeming "steadfast love" and "faithfulness." In biblical theology this theme culminates in the renewal of God's image in the person of Christ (Col. 3:10), who *is* the image of God (Col. 1:15).

David, the Penultimate Portrait of Yahweh's Condescension

In the Psalter we see stages of Yahweh's self-identity with humanity, an identity that theologically speaking is anchored in the creation of humankind in God's image, implying that God can never abandon humanity because it would be tantamount to abandoning himself.

Before we consider further the ultimate expressions of Yahweh's humbled estate among his human creatures, we should pay regard to the way the Psalter portrays David as the prototype of the "poor and needy." That is, Israel's ideal king, David, condescends from his regal estate to become the representative of the "poor and needy," and more than a representative, to become their epitome, repeatedly confessing, "I am poor and needy." This is a stage on the way to understanding Yahweh as the condescending God who enters the domain of the poor and needy, and from that humble estate, lifts them up to princedom. One of the theological realities of the Psalms is that David is the human figure who, more persistently than any other, is the presenter of Israel's and humanity's sinful state and then the representative of Israel redeemed. David is fallen humanity incarnate, perhaps best illustrated by Psalm 51, and redeemed humanity, illustrated by his identity with the poor and needy, the object of Yahweh's love. As we discussed in "Introductory Matters,"[5] at some point in the development of the Psalter, most likely in the wake of the exile and return, a theologically astute editor strategically placed David's confession, "I am poor and needy," in four passages of the Psalter. Occurring in all four books except Book 4, it is David's self-identity with his beloved nation Israel, in solidarity with his people in their low estate. James Luther Mays comments about the David connection: "The David of the psalms enacts and illustrates and teaches a life lived by the steadfast love of the Lord. In the David psalms this king of Israel is identified as, and identifies with the *'aniyyim*, the lowly who say to the Lord, 'I am poor and needy.' The connection with David does not so much claim the psalms as the voice of a king as it identifies him, in the psalms that are claimed for David, with the lowly."[6]

5. See "Theology from the Psalms" in "Introductory Matters."
6. Mays, *The Lord Reigns*, 123.

Psalm 144:3 raises the same question as 8:4: "O LORD, what is man that you regard him, or the son of man that you think of him?" The concern of the question is the brevity of human life—"his days are like a passing shadow" (144:4)—and prompted by pity, the psalmist prays that Yahweh will "bow your heavens, O LORD, and come down! . . . Rescue me and deliver me from the many waters, from the hand of foreigners, whose mouths speak lies and whose right hand is a right hand of falsehood" (vv. 5, 7–8, 11). The metaphor "bow your heavens" envisions God as moving from heaven to earth. It is both metaphorical and theological. The same is true of the two instances where Yahweh is enthroned, in the first instance on the "praises of Israel" (22:3) and in the second "upon the cherubim" in the temple (80:1).

These are pictures of Yahweh having already condescended to dwell in Israel's midst. They remind us that Yahweh's most common dwelling place in the earth is the temple where his presence abides (e.g., Pss. 26:8; 27:4). The point is that Yahweh is very much at home in the world he made and with the people he chose, at home because that is where he wants to be (see the covenant formula), and that is where he is needed. He shapes himself to the need of his people, not twisting himself out of shape to accommodate the poor and needy and oppressed—that's who he really is. The inclination and the power of the Lord's shaping is a reflex of his nature as the humbled and humbling God. Psalm 41:3 presents the imagery of Yahweh as a nurse or physician who enters the sick person's room and turns the patient's bed to refresh and restore him to health. Amos Hakham renders the sense of the verse thus: "You, O Lord, overturned his entire bed, in the manner of someone attending a sick person, who turns over the bed on which the sick person is lying, in order to clean and arrange it."[7] We do not see Yahweh condescending as such, but we see him in his already condescended estate, exercising his tender care in the sick room of his servants, one of the most beautiful portraits of the humbled Yahweh.

The point is that the portrait of the lowly Yahweh is a product of his true nature, and it is built into the plan of redemption (Phil. 2). It is from that humble estate, and only from that estate, says Augustine, that he lifts us up:

> I was not humble enough to possess Jesus in His humility as my God, nor did I know what lesson was taught by His weakness. For your Word, the eternal truth, high above the highest parts of your creation, raises up to itself those who are subdued, but in this lower world He built for Himself a humble dwelling

7. Hakham, *The Bible: Psalms*, 1:323.

out of our clay, by means of which He might detach from themselves those who were to be subdued and bring them over to Himself, healing the swelling of their pride and fostering their love, so that instead of going further in their own self-confidence they should put on weakness, seeing at their feet divinity in the weakness that it had put on by wearing our "coat of skin"; and then, weary, they should cast themselves down upon that divinity which, rising, would bear them up aloft.[8]

The Ultimate Portrait of Yahweh Who Condescends

We have already asserted that Book 5 of the Psalter (Pss. 107–50) is compiled against the background of the Babylonian exile, the exiles' return to Judea, and the rebuilding of the temple. Psalms 113–18 form a unit, called the Egyptian Hallel, that celebrates the return from exile and the reconstruction of the temple. Understandably, the exile was a period of national humiliation and a threat to Israel's future existence. Psalm 113, the first psalm in the unit, presents a portrait of the humbled Yahweh who, though exalted above the heavens, condescended to the humiliated "poor" (*dal*) and "needy" (*'ebyon*): "who humbleth himself [*mashpil*] to behold the things that are in heaven, and in the earth!" (v. 6 KJV); and further, who "raises the poor from the dust and lifts the needy from the ash heap, to make them sit with princes, with the princes of his people. He gives the barren woman a home, making her the joyous mother of children" (vv. 7–9).

Isaiah's description of the exalted and humbled Yahweh moves in the same vein of thought:

> For thus says the One who is high and lifted up,
>   who inhabits eternity, whose name is Holy:
> "I dwell in the high and holy place,
>   and also with him who is of contrite and lowly spirit,
> to revive the spirit of the lowly,
>   and to revive the heart of the contrite." (Isa. 57:15)

We have already observed that Psalm 113 shows Yahweh in the act of condescension as he "*stoops down* to look on the heavens and the earth" (NIV). Even though he *stoops down* to lift up "the poor from the dust" (Ps. 113:6, 7), Yahweh in no way relinquishes his sovereignty over the world. Yahweh's condescension

8. Augustine, *The Confessions of St. Augustine*, book 7, chap. 18 (p. 155).

was for the express purpose of restoring his people, humiliated by the exile, to the noble position of princedom, to engage the psalmist's metaphor.

The exalted and humbled Yahweh is also the subject of Psalm 138, the initial psalm in the final set of David psalms (Pss. 138–45). Unapologetically, David asserts faith in the exalted Yahweh, who is totally at home in his humbled estate and attends to his troubled servant:

> Though the Lord is exalted, he looks kindly on the lowly;
> though lofty, he sees them from afar.
> Though I walk in the midst of trouble,
> you preserve my life.
> You stretch out your hand against the anger of my foes;
> with your right hand you save me. (Ps. 138:6–7)

There is no wonder that "his understanding is beyond measure" (147:5), for the exalted and humbled God is one. Charles Spurgeon comments on our paradoxical God: "From stars to sighs is a deep descent! From worlds to wounds is a distance which only infinite compassion can bridge. Yet he who acts a surgeon's part with wounded hearts, marshals the heavenly host, and reads the muster roll of suns and the majestic system."[9]

Yahweh Revealed in Suffering and Weakness

Thus the humbled Yahweh in the Psalter is the theological equivalent of the Suffering Servant in Isaiah (Isa. 52:13–53:12) and the precursor of the suffering Savior in the New Testament. Books 3, 4, and 5 of the Psalter use the story of Exodus 32–34 (the golden calf and renewal of the covenant) as a template for the program of Israel's restoration from the Babylonian exile. After Moses requests of the Lord, "Please show me your glory" (Exod. 33:18), the Lord says to Moses, "You cannot see my face, for man shall not see me and live" (v. 20). The Lord continues with a different option: "There is a place by me where you shall stand on the rock, and while my glory passes by I will put you in a cleft in the rock, and I will cover you with my hand until I have passed by. Then I will take away my hand, and you shall see my back, but my face shall not be seen" (vv. 21–23). Based on this text, Martin Luther posits a "theology of the cross" over against a "theology of glory" and teaches that God's "back"

9. Spurgeon, *Treasury of David*, 3:415.

represents the hidden God (*Deus absconditus*), who is ultimately revealed in the cross. Paradoxically speaking, God makes the full revelation of himself in the suffering and ignominy of the cross. Theologian Bonnie Pattison has made a study of Luther's teaching on the theology of the cross and demonstrates, point by point, what others have also intimated, that Luther was John Calvin's teacher in this matter. Pattison states candidly (also quoting Alistar McGrath): "Luther taught that God's revelation is found only in suffering and in the cross, not in works or human moral acts. Luther maintained that the knowledge of God concealed in Christ 'shatters human illusions concerning the capacity of human reason to discern God' anywhere except 'in Christ crucified.'"[10]

While the exclusive right and mission of Yahweh's lifting up the humble are not exactly stated in Psalm 113, they are implied by the fact that this psalm, as we have pointed out, belongs to a collection (Pss. 113–18) compiled against the miraculous return of the exiles to their home in Judea (ca. 536 BC)—miraculous in that it was accomplished not by military power but by Cyrus's decree of 538 BC. In Yahweh's humbled estate—*stooping down* to look on the heavens and the earth (Ps. 113:6)—he spared his people, and their posterity would continue.

In his commentary on Genesis, Calvin speaks about the exclusive role of Christ's cross to reveal those things that are unknowable by our human senses and raise us "above the heavens": "Nothing shall we find, I say, above or below, which can raise us up to God, until Christ shall have instructed us in his own school. Yet this cannot be done, unless, we having emerged out of the lowest depths, are borne up above all heavens, in the chariot of his [Christ's] cross, that there by faith we may apprehend those things which the eye has never seen, the ear never heard, and which far surpass our hearts and minds."[11]

We can see how this doctrine produced the image, attributed to Calvin, of the suffering church traveling as a pilgrim through this world with bent back and overflowing tears, among these everlasting ruins (see Ps. 74:3).[12] The assumption of this image and spiritual demeanor is the only way we as individual believers and as Christ's church can know God in his full revelation, as Paul said: "that I may know him and the power of his resurrection, and may share his sufferings, becoming like him in his death" (Phil. 3:10). Indeed, the

10. Pattison, "The Suffering Church in Calvin's *De Scandalis*," 120; Pattison quotes McGrath, *Luther's Theology of the Cross*, 150.
11. Calvin, *Commentaries on the Book of Genesis*, 1:63.
12. Selderhuis, *John Calvin*, 162.

Lord has designed the plan of redemption in such a way that the suffering of Christ and the ignominy of the cross are the only way to salvation, and we are to replicate that model. The paradox is that the beauty of the church is revealed only through its suffering:

> However, let us remember that the outward aspect of the Church is so contempt-ible that its beauty may shine within; that it is so tossed about on earth that it may have a permanent dwelling-place in heaven; that it lies so wounded and broken in the eyes of the world that it may stand, vigorous and whole, in the presence of God and his angels; that it is so wretched in the flesh that its happiness may nevertheless be restored for it in the spirit. In the same way, when Christ lay despised in a stable, multitudes of angels were singing his excellence; the star in the heavens was giving proof of his glory; and the magi from a far-off land realized his significance. When he was hungry in the wilderness and when he was contending with the taunts of Satan to the point of sweating blood, the angels were once again ministering to him [Mark 1:13; Luke 22:43f.]. When he was just about to be fettered he drove back his enemies with his words alone [John 18:6]. When the sun failed, it was proclaiming him—hanging on the cross—King of the world; and the open tombs were acknowledging him Lord of death and life [Matt. 27:45, 52f.]. Now, if we see Christ in his own body crushed by cruel tyranny, exposed to derisive behavior, violently dragged this way and that, do not let us be frightened by any of those things, as if they were unusual. On the contrary, let us be convinced that the Church has been ordained for this purpose, that as long as it is a sojourner in the world it is to wage war under the perpetual cross.[13]

As Pattison reminds us, "The church is afflicted because Christ was afflicted. Like a true knowledge of Christ, a true knowledge of the church's condition is paradoxical, its real beauty and spiritual vitality is hidden under its weakness, brokenness and worldly contempt."[14]

The final word is well spoken by the apostle Paul when he commends the mind of Christ as the example for the Philippian church:

> In your relationships with one another, have the same mindset as Christ Jesus:
>> Who, being in very nature God,
>>> did not consider equality with God something to be used to his own advantage;

13. Calvin, *Concerning Scandals*, 29–30.
14. Pattison, "The Suffering Church in Calvin's *De Scandalis*," 9.

rather, he made himself nothing
    by taking the very nature of a servant,
    being made in human likeness.
And being found in appearance as a man,
    he humbled himself
    by becoming obedient to death—
        even death on a cross!
Therefore God exalted him to the highest place
    and gave him the name that is above every name,
that at the name of Jesus every knee should bow,
    in heaven and on earth and under the earth,
and every tongue acknowledge that Jesus Christ is Lord,
    to the glory of God the Father. (Phil. 2:5–11 NIV)

So it is on the pattern of Yahweh's suffering in the Psalter and elsewhere that Scripture bows its knees to the God who humbles himself to reveal his true and eternal nature. That means, as the Psalter strongly attests, that the Lord is with us in our lowest and most humbled moments of life and is present to lift us up. And as Paul asserts, this portrait of the true God, both exalted and humbled, is our model to imitate. James sums up the biblical commandment for all Christians: "Humble yourselves before the Lord, and he will exalt you" (James 4:10). Paul's word from the Lord when he contemplated his thorn in the flesh and its purpose in his life puts this colossal truth in a practical context: "My grace is sufficient for you, for my power is made perfect in weakness" (2 Cor. 12:9). This is a word of sufficient grace and sufficient assurance of the exalted God's condescension.

FIVE

Judgment, the Other Side of Justice

A Levitical Sanction of Yahweh's Claim (Ps. 73)

With the images of men wielding their axes to cut through the forest thicket, Psalm 74 visualizes the destruction of the temple (Ps. 74:4–8). Psalm 73, its neighbor and the opening psalm of Book 3, begins on the note of God's justice, which the psalmist found to be a formidable issue that created both complexity and envy within his soul. But his spiritual anguish paid generous dividends when he went into the temple and found a resolution, the assurance of God's judgment on the wicked: "then I discerned their end" (v. 17). Justice and judgment had come together in the psalmist's theological reflections, and the image of judgment was not pretty (vv. 18–20). Yet the psalmist had found that the resolution, the real resolution, was not envy but "to be near God" (v. 28). This Levitical poet,[1] who by God's own appointment had no landed property, recognized that his lot was the height of spiritual aspiration: the Lord was his portion! Our suppliant arrived at this robust view of God as one who is always present, holds him with his right hand, guides with his counsel, and will ultimately take him into glory (vv. 23–26).

This alternate view of God's all-embracing care—justice for the righteous—is one of the most beautiful and powerful descriptions of life with

---

1. Psalms 73–83 originate in the family of Asaph, a Levitical family whom David appointed to serve as musicians in the temple (1 Chron. 15:19–21).

God that we have in the Psalms. It is the "pearl of great price" that drew out of the psalmist's soul the exclamation of purest devotion: "And there is nothing on earth that I desire besides you" (Ps. 73:25). Here in this psalm the Lord's claim on the Levites, "The Levites are mine" (Num. 3:12 NIV), is answered by their inalienable claim on Yahweh: "Whom have I in heaven but you?" (Ps. 73:25). Transferring this claim to all believers, when the Lord claims us, he also offers himself as our inalienable portion.

Two Sides of the Same Coin

The idea of divine judgment is an obstacle for many people because they say, "How can a loving God punish the people he created?" While I do not want to diminish the importance of this question—it has some merits—there is another question that ought to be laid alongside it: "How can a loving God *not* punish the people he created who disobey his commandments which are designed for their betterment?" First of all, we should acknowledge that God has made generous provision for handling this problem: he has provided forgiveness for our sins. That gracious provision, of course, requires a recognition that we have violated God's commandments, and such a breach is a violation of his own person, of God's gracious character: "Against you, you only, have I sinned and done what is evil in your sight, so that you may be justified in your words and blameless in your judgment" (Ps. 51:4). David does not mean that his family and friends and country were not affected by his sin—indeed they were!—but when his sins were all weighed on the scales of justice, the one violated, most violated, was God. God's commandments are a reflection of his character, and when we violate them we defame God's character. Jesus reminded us that the two fundamental commandments are to love God with all our being and to love our neighbor as ourselves: "You shall love the Lord your God with all your heart and with all your soul and with all your mind. This is the great and first commandment. And a second is like it: You shall love your neighbor as yourself. On these two commandments depend all the Law and the Prophets" (Matt. 22:37–40). Even if our humanistic world finds loving God a negligible obligation, they should nevertheless marvel at the instruction to love our neighbor as ourselves. However, if they do not keep the first commandment, they will likely falter in keeping the second. Believers understandably marvel at both commandments and their comprehensive design.

To speak to our metaphor of two sides of the same coin, the question is whether a system of justice can be defended if it does not recognize the need for accountability. Accountability is endemic to any system of justice, a recognition of both right and wrong. In the Psalms and the Bible generally accountability is indemnified by reward and punishment, sometimes expressed as blessings and curses. Obeying the commandments brings blessings (reward), and violating the commandments brings curses (punishment). As we have emphasized over and over again in our study, God reveals his character in the commandments and covenants. The formula of grace in Exodus 34:6–7 is one of the best illustrations. Yahweh is "a God merciful and gracious, slow to anger, and abounding in steadfast love and faithfulness, keeping steadfast love for thousands, forgiving iniquity and transgression and sin, but who will by no means clear the guilty, visiting the iniquity of the fathers on the children and the children's children, to the third and fourth generation" (Exod. 34:6–7).

If we find the punishment of the children for their parents' sins troublesome, we only have to look to Deuteronomy and Ezekiel for the basic adjustment of that principle: "Fathers shall not be put to death because of their children, nor shall children be put to death because of their fathers. Each one shall be put to death for his own sin" (Deut. 24:16; cf. Ezek. 18:1–18). Related to our basic question, however, if God rewards the righteous and does not punish the wicked, where would equity be found in that system? Forgiveness, as we have acknowledged, is God's corrective, but it is accompanied by our sense of regret that we have offended God's law, which is another way of saying we have offended God's Person. We are not talking about a vengeful God. Even in our Western system of jurisprudence, which prescribes punishment for offenders, we do not consider it vengeful. Rather, it is justice, a mark of accountability.

At the same time, we do not want to diminish the gravity of the kind of punishment that seems to defy the boundaries of just punishment. The Psalms repeat in various ways the assurance that God is just, and that means he is fair in doling out reward and punishment. He is compassionate and gracious, and we need to lay out the theory of divine justice alongside its practical applications as given in the Psalms and as we have seen it demonstrated in our own lives. When we do, lamentably, there will be instances when divine punishment seems to overstep the bounds of justice. Christians have tended to explain the absence of justice or the excessive exercise of punishment, both in Scripture and in our personal lives, as instances when we must wait for the eschatological hope of absolute justice, in terms of both reward and punishment.

Yet, perhaps our minds resort too quickly to the world to come as a means to even out the score. There is nothing wrong with siding, at least temporarily, with James Russell Lowell's poem, "Truth forever on the scaffold, Wrong forever on the throne"[2]—that's the world we live in—but we must also insist that this is an expression of our hope in God's just ways. If it takes eternity to put the system into perfect synchronism, that's really a decision God must make. When I am trying to comfort those who believe that the system has not served up a just verdict, I am reluctant to hurry along to the world-to-come explanation, and sometimes it is best to resort to an agnostic position that there is so much we don't understand about God's system of justice and how it moves along. God distributes his mercy in various ways and various quantities to individuals and nations. In that context we have to focus on the One who stands behind the system.

Psalm 75 instructs us in some particulars. First, the psalmist assures us that God has set a time for equitable judgment (v. 2), which in this psalm seems to be this world and not the world to come. Thus we can wait for justice in this world, and that can help us to live with—not accept, but live with—the injustice of this world. Martin Luther recognized that God sometimes hides his justice: "God hides his power in weakness, his wisdom in folly, his goodness in severity, his justice in sins, his mercy in anger."[3] God is still in control of a world filled with distorted systems of justice, past and present, and he is still working the system to produce the proper result: "it is God who executes judgment, putting down one and lifting up another" (v. 7). And we can be sure that the outcome is deferential to the righteous who reflect God's character.

The Distributive Pattern of Justice and Judgment (Pss. 75 and 58)

Psalm 74:22 is a prayer that God will arise and defend his cause, especially since he has been the object of mockery in a world that does not honor him. Psalm 75 is, in part at least, the answer to that prayer. But the action is not arbitrary, for God judges "uprightly" (75:2). In a world that often looks like it has been shaped by Lowell's witticism quoted above, we can so easily despair

2. Lowell, "The Present Crisis."
3. Quoted by Bainton, *Here I Stand*, 48.

that justice is a rare commodity. Psalm 58, like Psalm 75, is a reminder that God still enacts his system of justice in the world, rewarding the righteous and punishing the wicked. It is a word of judgment spoken to rulers who are the purveyors of injustice: "Sooner than your pots can feel the heat of thorns, whether green or ablaze, may he sweep them away! . . . Mankind will say, 'Surely there is a reward for the righteous; surely there is a God who judges on earth'" (Ps. 58:9, 11).

Of a certainty, God metes out punishment and reward, and it is not arbitrary but determined by the behavior of the earth's inhabitants and by the divine standard of accountability. If God did not punish the guilty and unrepentant, he would not be a fair judge.

God's Absolute Sovereignty (Pss. 93–100)

When we speak of the sovereignty of God, we mean that God rules over every aspect of the universe. To be absolutely sovereign, he must hold absolute authority over every aspect of the created order. The psalms of the heavenly King (Pss. 93–100) bring all of those dimensions under Yahweh's sovereign rule and reign: sovereign over the gods, if such exist (96:4–6; 97:7, 9); sovereign over every thing and every movement of creation (93:1–3; 96:1–5, 10–13; 97:9; 98:7–9); sovereign over all the nations of the earth (97:1, 5–7; 98:2, 4, 9); and sovereign in justice (96:10–13; 97:2, 6; 99:4) and judgment (96:13; 97:8; 98:9).

Quickly the attendant problem arises for us as it did for Job and Ecclesiastes and the psalmists: If God is sovereign in all these aspects of creation, why is injustice sometimes served on the innocent? Why did Israel suffer defeat when they were loyal to God (Ps. 44), and why did Job lose everything, including his children and health, when he was innocent? John Calvin and Franz Delitzsch, among other scholars, consider the psalms of the heavenly King to be a description of the messianic kingdom, since the picture is far better than the earthly picture Israel knew.[4] The differential between the earthly and the ideal kingdoms presses interpreters in the direction of this interpretive method. They insist, and I think rightly, that the differential between the present reality of God's kingdom on earth as we know it and the coming kingdom as these psalms describe it (Pss. 96:1–13; 98:7–9) can only be a picture of the

---

4. Calvin, *Commentary on the Book of Psalms*, 4:47; Delitzsch, *Biblical Commentary on the Psalms*, 3:34.

eschatological kingdom when heaven's voices announce: "The kingdom of the world has become the kingdom of our Lord and of his Messiah, and he will reign for ever and ever" (Rev. 11:15). While the critics of the biblical idea of judgment may indict us on this point, it is nevertheless an integral part of the faith we confess, and we should not apologize for it or diminish its confessional prominence, although we should use it wisely.

SIX

Covenant, the Intractable Bond

The Mosaic Covenant in the Psalter

The covenant between Yahweh and Israel is intractable. God is a bold God. The first hint of that is in Genesis 1, where he creates humanity in his own image, a resolute gesture that reveals his commitment to this new creation and his identity with them. Reflecting this bold love and commitment, the covenant with Israel is an expression of Yahweh's character as operative in Israel and the human family.

Generally speaking, the formula of grace in the second Sinai covenant (Exod. 34:6–7) has already merited much attention in our study, and that for good reason: it is the pervading profile of Yahweh in the Psalms.[1] It constitutes the underpinnings of all that happens between Yahweh and Israel—and the world—and Yahweh's character description in the formula of grace is the defining modus operandi. The Mosaic covenant, made with Israel after

---

1. I have noted all the verses of the Psalter where the two terms of the formula of grace (*hesed* and *'emet* [or *'emunah*]) appear in one verse or within two verses of each other, which I consider as an allusion (references to the Hebrew versification are provided in brackets). **Book 1**: 26:3; 40:12. **Book 2**: 37:3[4], 10[11]; 61:7[8]; 69:13[14], 16[17] (in the last verse, "abundance of your mercies" [*rob rahameka*] appears rather than "faithfulness" [*'emet/'emunah*]). **Book 3**: 85:10[11]; 86:15; 88:11[12]; 89:1[2], 14[15], 24[25], 33[34], 49[50]. **Book 4**: 92:2[3]; 98:3; 100:6; 103:8. **Book 5**: 111:4; 112:4; 115:1; 116:5; 117:2; 145:8. The three direct quotations of Exod. 34:6 are 86:15; 103:8; and 145:8.

their golden calf debacle, is the fundamental and intractable bond between Yahweh and Israel—intractable because God created humankind in his own image and out of his own grace called Abraham and his descendants as his special people, appointing them to bless the world: "He remembers his covenant forever, the word that he commanded, for a thousand generations, the covenant that he made with Abraham, his sworn promise to Isaac, which he confirmed to Jacob as a statute, to Israel as an everlasting covenant, saying: 'To you I will give the land of Canaan as your portion for an inheritance'" (Ps. 105:8–11).

Even in those Psalms when the Lord's patience seems to run out, he acts on Israel's behalf for his own name's sake: "Our fathers, when they were in Egypt, did not consider your wondrous works; they did not remember the abundance of your steadfast love, but rebelled by the sea, at the Red Sea. Yet he saved them *for his name's sake*, that he might make known his mighty power" (Ps. 106:7–8).

And there are critical moments of history when Yahweh, moved by his people's cry of distress, saves them—because he loves them: "Many times he delivered them, but they were rebellious in their purposes and were brought low through their iniquity. Nevertheless, he looked upon their distress when he heard their cry. For their sake he remembered his covenant, and relented *according to the abundance of his steadfast love*" (Ps. 106:43–45).[2]

Profile Shaping as a Literary/Theological Method

In biblical prophecy and in much of the Psalter, the hope of the coming age, the kingdom of God, rises out of the ashes of the old age and takes the heroes, institutions, and unfulfilled hopes of a former age as the types, renewed and enhanced, of the age to come. On this kingdom the Psalter often focuses its gaze. Outside the Psalms, an example of reduplicating a former age is Ezekiel's description of a new temple and the reconfiguration of Israel's tribal claims (Ezek. 40–48). That is to say, the new age is often a reshaping of the old.

In the Old Testament generally and the Psalms particularly, Moses is the model profile. The framework of the Former Prophets (Joshua, Judges,

---

2. Psalm 106 surveys Yahweh's actions on Israel's behalf by dealing with four historical paradigms: (1) the miracle at the Red Sea (vv. 8–12); (2) apostasy of the golden calf (vv. 19–23); (3) apostasy at Baal-peor (vv. 30–31); and (4) "many times," a general assessment of Yahweh's historical actions (vv. 43–45). See Bullock, *Psalms*, 2:257–58.

1–2 Samuel, and 1–2 Kings) reinforces this analogy of Moses. The writer of Joshua was aware that Moses's mantle had been passed on to this new leader: "Just as I was with Moses, so I will be with you" (Josh. 1:5). Yet Joshua's leadership, in the flow of the book, had not been established in the eyes of Israel. The story thus unfolds in such a way as to give it a Mosaic imprint. When the Israelites had miraculously crossed the Jordan River, the Mosaic imprimatur was stamped on Joshua as Israel's leader: "On that day the LORD exalted Joshua in the sight of all Israel, and they stood in awe of him *just as they had stood in awe of Moses*, all the days of his life" (Josh. 4:14; cf. Exod. 14:31). Further, when Joshua faced the challenge of Jericho, the commander of the Lord's army instructed him, "Take off your sandals from your feet, for the place where you are standing is holy" (Josh. 5:15), just as the Lord had commanded Moses to take off his shoes at the burning bush (Exod. 3:1–6).

Also in the Former Prophets the prophet Elijah is described in much the same way (1 Kings 17–19).[3] Frank Moore Cross makes this case very clearly. Elijah, like Moses before him, was the key to the survival of the faith of Yahweh. So the writer of Kings carefully tells the story of Elijah as the *new Moses*. First Kings 18 and 19 form the account of Elijah on Mount Carmel, and the narrative is framed in such a way as to suggest that this was the "second" revelation on Mount Sinai given to a "second" Moses. In broad outline, Elijah's translation to heaven in the Transjordan opposite Jericho is reminiscent of Moses's death (2 Kings 2), and the miraculous parting of the Jordan River by Elijah (2 Kings 2:8) directs the reader's attention back to Moses's parting of the Red Sea (Exod. 14:21–25). The story of Elijah on Mount Carmel provides even more specific parallels with Moses on Mount Sinai. First, as Moses built an altar at Sinai and set up twelve stones to represent the twelve tribes of Israel (Exod. 24:4), so Elijah builds an altar of twelve stones "according to the number of the tribes of the sons of Jacob" (1 Kings 18:31). Second, when Moses descended from the mountain and found the golden calf affair in progress, he demanded that Israel decide between their idol and Yahweh, "Who is on the LORD's side? Come to me" (Exod. 32:26). Then Moses and the Levites engaged in killing the devotees of the golden calf (Exod. 32:27–28). In a similar action, Elijah calls upon the Israelites to decide between Baal and Yahweh, "How long will you go limping between two different opinions? If the LORD is God, follow him; but if Baal, then follow him" (1 Kings 18:21).

---

3. Cross, *Canaanite Myth and Hebrew Epic*, 190–94.

Then after the contest Elijah executes the prophets of Baal (1 Kings 18:40). The purpose of this profiling strategy for the writer of Kings is to cast Elijah in the profile of Moses as reformer of the faith, as the prophet like Moses (Deut. 18:15) who rescued Israel from idolatry.

Recasting David in the Persona of Moses

The Psalms carry out this literary/theological method in subtle ways, much like the writer of Kings, and the figure of Moses again is the most prominent person for profiling purposes. Generally Moses's name is left to the reader's/listener's memory as it is in the story of Elijah in 1 Kings 17–19. An example in the Psalter is Psalm 27, where David uses Yahweh's words that instructed Joshua to assume leadership after Moses's death (cf. Josh. 1:6, 7, 9 and Ps. 27:14; Josh. 1:5 and Ps. 27:9). As noted above, the writer of Joshua casts Joshua as a Moses-like figure (cf. Josh. 4:14 and Exod. 14:26–31; Josh. 5:15 and Exod. 3:3).

Similarly, David is brought under the theological umbrella of the Mosaic covenant, in part, by recasting him in the persona of Moses. As indicated earlier,[4] an editor positioned the formula of grace (Exod. 34:6), the heart of the second Sinai revelation, in three strategic places in the last three books of the Psalter, accomplishing a remarkable objective. He made sure that David was viewed under the auspices of the Mosaic covenant and, like Joshua, as the recipient of Moses's mantle of leadership. The purpose of the quotation of the formula of grace in Psalm 86:15, I proposed, was to prepare the listeners of the Psalms for the challenging question of Psalm 89:49: "Lord, where is your former great love [hesed], which in your faithfulness ['emunah] you swore to David?" (NIV). So when we encounter the question of the ostensible failure of the Davidic covenant in Psalm 89, we have already heard David's voice in Psalm 86—the only David psalm in Book 3—affirming Yahweh's love and faithfulness tendered in the second Sinai covenant. David was a Mosaic believer!

Intertextually, we should observe that David prays the formula of grace in Psalm 86:15 just as Moses did in his prayer of intercession for Israel when the Lord had said he would disinherit Israel and raise up a nation from Moses (Num. 14). David, now frocked in the mantle of Moses and praying the words of the formula of grace, affirms Yahweh's covenant with Moses and Israel,

---

4. See "Theology from the Psalms" in "Introductory Matters."

proclaiming that Yahweh was faithful to keep his promises: "But you, O Lord, are a God merciful and gracious, slow to anger and abounding in steadfast love [*hesed*] and faithfulness [*'emet*]" (Ps. 86:15).

David's Implicit Confession of the Formula of Grace (Ps. 25)

David's quotation of the formula of grace three times in the Psalter[5] amounts to casting David in a Moses-like profile. Obviously this is an explicit use of the formula, but Psalm 25 represents an implicit use of the formula. That is, it employs the nomenclature of covenant and reinforces the implicit presence of covenant with explicit terms.

First, the verbs of Psalm 25 spell out the function of the covenant: "show/ make known" (*yd'*, v. 4a); "teach" (*lmd*, vv. 4b, 5, 9); "guide" (*drk*, vv. 5, 9); "instruct" (*yrh*, v. 12). Without mentioning the term "covenant," David nevertheless invokes the covenant as the source (instruction) and means (guidance) of living.

Second, we should observe that the specific terms of covenant are not missing in the psalm. Both expressions "his [Yahweh's] covenant" and "his [Yahweh's] testimonies" occur in verse 10 (also "covenant" in v. 14), enforcing the idea that David, without mentioning it by name up to this point in the psalm, has been speaking of the covenant all along. But what covenant is David talking about? The answer becomes evident when we recognize that this psalm has the formula of grace written all over it. This is where we have to be very perceptive regarding the psalmists' use of scriptural echoes (see "Reflecting on Methodology" in Introductory Matters).

Psalm 25, in fact, echoes Exodus 34:6–7 by using the major terms of the formula of grace: "steadfast love" (*hesed*), "faithfulness" (*'emet*), "mercy" (*rahameka*), "sins" (*hatta'ot*), "transgressions" (*pesha'im*), and "forgive" (*nasa'*). In other words, the vocabulary of the formula of grace is the glossary that David uses to write his psalm and thus reveal the covenant he has in mind. The ancient readers/listeners probably had the formula in their memories, and they would have recognized the connection. The point is that Psalm 25 illustrates the implicit formula of grace, the heart of the second Sinai covenant, revealing the covenant that undergirds David's spiritual commitment. We can see, then, that covenant, despite the Psalter's long compilation history, is part of the theological infrastructure, often articulated clearly but more often

5. Book 3, Ps. 86:15; Book 4, Ps. 103:8; Book 5, Ps. 145:8.

written between the lines of these 150 psalms. Like "steadfast love" (*hesed*) in the Psalter, it governs the religious life of Israel even when its names and terms are not covenant-specific.

David's Appeal to the Formula of Grace (Ps. 86; Num. 14)

The Mosaic covenant describes Yahweh's character, and the Davidic covenant, which receives explicit treatment only twice in the Psalter (Pss. 89 and 132), illustrates God's compassionate and faithful nature to fulfill the promises to his chosen rulers. To illustrate how Moses himself uses the formula of grace, we have only to listen to his intercessory prayer for Israel when they, having rejected the report of the spies, complain against Moses and Aaron and say they will choose another leader and return to Egypt. Moses appeals to the formula of grace in his plea for Yahweh to forgive the people for their transgression (Num. 14:19). That is what Yahweh had promised to do, and the formula of grace in Books 3, 4, and 5 of the Psalms functions as a Mosaic promise, now portended to David, and builds upon Yahweh's intractable love (*hesed*) and faithfulness (*'emet*). And that reassurance, measured against the historical context of the end of the Davidic dynasty (Ps. 89), constitutes the sustaining hope of that era of uncertainty. But it also casts David, like Moses, in an intercessory role against those who opposed him (Ps. 86:14–15). Psalm 86 reflects the intercessory ministry of Moses and his love for his people as a literary convention and a theological affirmation by casting David in the same profile. There was no better person than David to bring hope to this despairing people.

David's Identification with His People: "I Am Poor and Needy"

David's identification with his beloved Israel is of momentous importance, for both the psalmists and the editor(s) of the Psalter. The identity theme appears in obvious form as David speaks in his own voice, "I am poor and needy" (Ps. 86:1), and borrows Moses's voice to confess his faith: "But you, O Lord, are a God merciful and gracious, slow to anger and abounding in steadfast love and faithfulness" (Ps. 86:15; cf. Exod. 34:6; see also above "Profile Shaping as a Literary/Theological Method"). Speculatively speaking, Psalm 90 could have concluded the poor-and-needy motif, especially since Moses's powerful and authoritative voice commences Book 4. Psalm 90, in fact, lauds Yahweh's presence with Israel, even amid the disaster that ended the Davidic dynasty and thrust Israel into seventy years of exile. By this psalm's juxtaposition to Psalm 89, the editor of Book 4 puts the tragic end of David's dynasty in the light of dwelling in God's secure presence, assured by none other than Moses himself. That assurance would have been enough to place Israel, with its intermingled history of trouble and triumph, in the care of their almighty God and leave the matter there. But judging from the editorial position of Psalm 109,[6] the editor of Book 5 sees the need as well as the opportunity to pronounce Yahweh's grace as the final arbiter of history (see "God's Love, the Shaper and Victor of History" in chap. 2).

So the editor stations David in the court of law, confessing: "I am poor and needy" (Ps. 109:22). Yahweh, Judge and Arbiter of history, takes his position at David's right hand to declare David innocent and victor over all his enemies. The foes of Israel, of David, and of God have "pursued the poor and needy and the brokenhearted, to put them to death" (109:16)—that's a brief assessment of Israel's wretched story. But the final word, after so many years and so many prayers, awaited David. None else but Yahweh himself had stepped into the Judge's place and pronounced the ultimate word of grace (109:31). Victory at last!

David's identification with his people mirrors Moses, who entreated the Lord to blot him out of his book, if indeed that was what Yahweh intended to do to erring Israel as a punishment for their sin of idolatry (Exod. 32:32–33). By his confession "I am poor and needy" in four different places of the Psalter (Pss. 40:17; 70:5; 86:1; 109:22), David becomes the prototype of suffering Israel as he shares their humiliated state in life and their ultimate victory over their enemies. For a book that begins with the profile of a king harassed and persecuted by his enemies within and without (Pss. 3–41), David's recurring prayers for deliverance from his enemies are finally answered in Psalm 109. And the answer is all the more impressive and conclusive when we see the Lord taking his place in the court of justice at the right hand of the needy to exonerate him, displacing David's numberless accusers: "For he [Yahweh] stands at the right hand of the needy one ['ebyon—David and the beloved

---

6. Contextually, I see the thrust of the opening psalms of Book 5 as accomplishing, at least in part, the following purposes: Ps. 107 sets Book 5 in the context of the return from exile (107:2–3); Ps. 108 is a psalm of thanksgiving that celebrates the new era now opening up for the nation (108:1–4); Ps. 109 pronounces David's ultimate and long-awaited victory over his enemies (see my comments on these psalms in *Psalms*, 2:283). For the significance of Yahweh's position at the "right hand of the needy one" (109:31), see my comments on Ps. 109:6 in *Psalms*, 2:286.

nation he represents], to save his life from those who would condemn him to death" (Ps. 109:31 AT). Just as David confessed his faith in the steadfast love (*hesed*) of Yahweh in 86:15, it is the same confident faith in Yahweh's love that underwrites the final verdict of victory in Psalm 109 (vv. 21, 25).

King David's Confession as "Servant"

In addition to David's confession, "I am poor and needy," Psalm 86 reinforces another of the powerful witnesses to David's humbled position before Yahweh by referring to him three times as "your [Yahweh's] servant" (86:2, 4, 16), an appellation that predominates in Book 5. Thus, in the only David psalm of Book 3, David depicts himself under the second Sinai covenant of Exodus 34:6–7 (Ps. 86:15), forming, in the larger sweep of Books 3, 4, and 5, an inclusio with the formula's closing quotation in Psalm 145:8, the final David psalm of the Psalter. In both Psalm 86 and the quotation of Psalm 89:49 the two covenants intersect, putting the Davidic covenant and Israel's beloved king under the auspices of the second Sinai covenant. Most likely that same editorial hand installed the other two instances of the formula (Pss. 103:8 and 145:8), putting a theological earmark on Books 3, 4, and 5. This edition of the Psalms, made by an anonymous editor, brought covenant renewal and fresh hope to a people who had been humiliated by the Babylonian conquest of 586 BC and the loss of the Davidic dynasty.[7]

The Covenant of Yahweh's Back and the Forbidden Covenant of Yahweh's Face (Exod. 33:17-20)

I am taking a bit of liberty here by naming the second Sinai covenant as "Yahweh's back" and the unconstituted covenant denied Moses as "Yahweh's face," but the reason should become clear as the conversation moves along. The Mosaic covenant (second Sinai) followed that critical moment in Israel's history when the Lord had miraculously delivered Israel from their four-hundred-year bondage in Egypt. The situation they faced was Moses's forty-day absence when he was on Mount Sinai receiving the first covenant. His absence tested their religious devotion, a test they failed miserably when they collaborated with Aaron to make a golden calf. Daunted by Yahweh's declaration that he would abolish Israel and not go with them into the land of Canaan, Moses

---

7. See Bullock, "Covenant Renewal and the Formula of Grace."

appealed to Yahweh not to destroy Israel and thus ruin the reputation he had earned by delivering them from Egypt (Exod. 32:11–14). When the Lord graciously relented, Moses pleaded with Yahweh to show him Yahweh's glory, which led to the second Sinai revelation, which we call the formula of grace (Exod. 34:6–7). Yahweh's response to Moses's request was that he would make his "goodness (tob/tub) pass by Moses and would proclaim his name Yahweh ("the LORD") while he covered Moses with his hand (33:19). Then Yahweh would remove his hand and Moses could see his "back" but not his "face" (33:23). We should note that Yahweh's "glory" (kabod) and Yahweh's "face" are used synonymously in this text (vv. 18, 20, 23), for when Yahweh responded to Moses's request to see Yahweh's glory, he said, "You cannot see my face, for man shall not see me and live" (v. 20). The idea behind the metaphor of "Yahweh's face" is that this is the revelation of God in his fullness, at least as full as human creatures could ever comprehend in their earthly condition. Above I have used the phrase "the forbidden covenant of Yahweh's face" to indicate that Moses had asked for more than a glance at Yahweh's back, as attested by the synonymous use of "glory" and "face."[8]

The question left for us, then, is, What does seeing Yahweh's "back" rather than his "face" entail? The essence of the anticipated epiphany is that Yahweh would proclaim his name Yahweh, and that is precisely what he did in the formula of grace: "The LORD passed before him [Moses] and proclaimed, 'The LORD, the LORD, a God merciful and gracious, slow to anger, and abounding in steadfast love and faithfulness, keeping steadfast love for thousands, forgiving iniquity and transgression and sin, but who will by no means clear the guilty, visiting the iniquity of the fathers on the children and the children's children, to the third and the fourth generation'" (Exod. 34:6–7).

The hermeneutical deduction is that seeing Yahweh's "back" is equivalent to the proclamation of Yahweh's name and character in the formula of grace, the essence of the "covenant of Yahweh's back." That is, Yahweh's self-revelation in the formula of grace was the truth behind the metaphor of "Yahweh's back." It falls in the category of argument that is known in rabbinic

---

8. In David's prayer in Ps. 4:6, "Lift up the light of your face upon us" (cf. Num. 6:25; Pss. 67:1; 80:3, 7, 19), the sense of the phrase "light of your face" is the Lord's favor; similarly, the Lord "hides" his face in Deut. 31:17–18 and 32:20. The Lord's intimate relationship to Moses is described by the phrase "face to face" in Deut. 5:4 and 34:10. In 2 Chron. 7:14 the Lord's words "seek my face" mean to pray. None of these uses measure up to the meaning of "face" in Exod. 33, where it carries the nuance of the supreme fullness of God's presence.

exegesis as *qal vahomer* ("minor to major"), sometimes called the simple to the complex, an argument that Christ himself used: "Or which one of you, if his son asks him for bread, will give him a stone? Or if he asks for a fish, will give him a serpent? If you then, who are evil, know how to give good gifts to your children, how much more will your Father who is in heaven give good things to those who ask him!" (Matt. 7:9–11).

The expression "how much more" is a typical way to express the comparison involved in the *qal vahomer* argument, and in our present case we might say it like this: since Yahweh's "back," the profile we humans can comprehend, is that of our God who is merciful and gracious, slow to anger, abounding in steadfast love and faithfulness, maintaining steadfast love to thousands, and forgiving wickedness, rebellion, and sin, then *how much more* will be the epiphany when "the upright shall behold his face" (Ps. 11:7; cf. 17:15). The hidden character of God that we humans cannot comprehend, at least in our present state, constitutes the ultimate formula of spiritual transcendence. John's language moves in the direction of that supreme expression, although he still does not throw back the curtain, even though he informs us that in the eschatological future it will be a reality when the story of redemption climaxes around the throne of God: "The throne of God and of the Lamb will be in the city, and his servants will serve him. *They will see his face* . . ." (Rev. 22:3–4 NIV). Of course, we can understand the *how much more* to have been revealed to us in Jesus Christ, who said to Philip, "Whoever has seen me has seen the Father" (John 14:9). Yet, in view of the statement in John's Apocalypse, we should wonder if John does not mean that there is yet another portion of glory awaiting us, not in addition to the lovely face of Jesus Christ, but a live encounter with the Father in the face of Jesus Christ. As I attempt to write words that might even approximate the truth and reality of that encounter, the words themselves seem to skip like rams before the very thought of the reality of seeing God's face (see Ps. 114:3–6).

SEVEN

The Laughter of God

Bold Metaphors and Their Truth Value

The Psalms are not adverse to using bold metaphors to describe God. For example, Psalm 78 deals with the Lord's exasperation with Israel's long and audacious disobedience as opposed to God's long and unrelenting commitment of love. And the metaphor describing God's response is as shocking as Israel's audacious disobedience—that is, God is depicted as an inebriated warrior breaking out of a drunken stupor, shouting at his enemies and putting them on the run (Ps. 78:65–66). There is no bolder metaphor about God in the Psalms.

We should read metaphors in the Bible for their delivery of truth, and we must also be careful not to overread them. In this case, we would never expect God to be inebriated (nor is the metaphor an excuse for overindulging in alcohol). Rather the truth of the metaphor depicts God's brazen yet defensive reaction to his children's disobedience and the judgment they had experienced as a result. God was fed up, to use my own bold metaphor, and he took drastic action. That's the truth value. The action amounted to a realignment of his plan: God rejected the tribe of Ephraim, born to the family line of Jacob's favorite wife, Rachel; he chose the tribe of Judah, born to Jacob's less favorite wife, Leah, and he chose David, a member of the tribe of Judah, who "shepherded them [Israel] with integrity of heart; with skillful hands he led them" (Ps. 78:72 NIV).

Motives for Laughter

Psalm 2 also presents a strong metaphor, quite different from Psalm 78 but similar in boldness: God laughs. Actually, the Psalter speaks of God's laughter three times: 2:4; 37:13; and 59:8.

We know there are many motives for laughter, and they form quite a wide range, which we can illustrate only in a limited way here. One is that things or circumstances just don't fit together in a logical pattern, and the incongruity creates a chuckle. We might say it tickles our funny bone, itself a metaphor. In the play *Henry IV, Part 1*, Shakespeare engages Scripture humorously, especially in the levity of his character Falstaff, whom Thomas Marc Parrott calls "one of the supreme achievements of Shakespeare's genius."[1] The memorable profile of Falstaff is that of a fat old man, fond of alcohol, and a gentleman by birth, but having become a highway robber by vocation. In one scene the Prince of Wales (Hal, the future King Henry IV of England) quips to Falstaff, "I see a good amendment of life in thee; from praying to purse-taking." And Falstaff rejoins: "Why, Hal, 'tis my vocation," to which the prince counters with an allusion to Ephesians 4:1, and probably a wink of the eye: "'Tis no sin for a man to labour in his vocation." To put Falstaff's comments in the biblical context, the apostle Paul was commending a life of moral integrity to the Ephesians: "Pray you that ye walk worthie of the vocation whereunto ye are called" (Eph. 4:1, the Geneva Bible). The incongruity of Paul's intention and Hal's application—a morally respectable life juxtaposed with a life of thievery—creates the humor.

In this same category, the manipulation of language can create laughter. We use a word that our hearers know very well, but they hear, or at least think, not the word we intend but a homonym whose variant spelling carries a different meaning. For example, "The professor always has the good *sense* to make her students comfortable." When the students hear that, they immediately think about the pleasant *scents* of the perfume she always wears. And a soft vibration of laughter drifts across the room.

Another example is a circumstance or prediction that is, for all practical purposes, impossible. This is true in Abraham's case when the Lord informed him that he, at age ninety-nine, and Sarah, at ninety, would have a child: "Then

---

1. For a brief description of Falstaff, see Thomas Marc Parrott's introduction to *The First Part of Henry the Fourth*, 344. The conversation between Hal and Falstaff is in *Henry IV, Part 1*, act 1, scene 2, lines 116–17, p. 351.

Abraham fell on his face and laughed" (Gen. 17:17). The motive that brought the physical response was the incompatibility of two nonagenarians having a child. Incongruence creates the humor.

At the other end of the spectrum is the kind of laughter we are all familiar with, joyful laughter that is generated by circumstances or thoughts that make us happy. In this case, the event or the thought and the physical response are in agreement. That is, the emotional response is triggered by something so delightful that it bubbles over into the physical response of laughter. That is the sense of those returning from Babylonian exile, filled with joy: "Our mouth was filled with laughter" (Ps. 126:2).

Laughter in Psalm 2:4

The reason for God's laughter in the Psalms is a little more complicated. It is the laughter we sometimes call having the last laugh—that is, when someone thinks they have gotten the best of us, but then fortune turns in our favor. Their intent does not match the outcome and is, in fact, quite the contrary. While we acknowledge that such laughter is sometimes vengeful, in God's case this is not so. Rather the laughter is generated by God's self-knowledge of his sovereign control over the world and human affairs that fall outside human expectation, maybe even human imagination. It is God effecting his will in human history, defeating the opposing forces of evil, even though the perpetrators, captive to their false assumptions, expect a different outcome. They overestimate their power and underestimate God's. All three instances of God's laughter in the Psalms reflect this reason for laughter. Evil nations or evil people think they have one up on God, and God laughs, derisively but not irreverently, at their ill-conceived and ill-performed actions, and most of all, their ill-formed notion of God and his power. It is a mocking laughter, the kind that says, "You thought you got the best of me, but I showed you in the end who's really in charge."

God's will on a cosmic scale, and also on a personal scale, generated from his steadfast love, is the final arbiter of redeeming history. The answer to the first question of the Heidelberg Catechism reads, in part: "He also watches over me in such a way that not a hair can fall from my head without the will of my Father in heaven; in fact, all things must work together for my salvation." When the kings of the earth had planned their rebellion against the "Lord and against his Anointed" (Ps. 2:2), the one "who sits in the heavens laughs" (v. 4). We might say it is analogous to a toddling child who believes she can do whatever her mother can do, and when the effort is expended, the child indeed perceives that it is accomplished, but the mother laughs because she sees the vast difference between the childish effort and her own adult capability. The problem is in both the perception and the performance, a problem which only the mother has a full perspective on. The element that is absent in the analogy is audacity—the child lovingly, not audaciously like the kings, wants to achieve the mother's physical dexterity. It is motivated by love, whereas the kings of the earth are motivated by thirst for power and control. But the redeeming factor is the alternative directive; the rebel kings are directed to "be wise" and "kiss the Son" (vv. 10, 12)—that is, submit to the sovereign rule of the One who sits in the heavens.

Laughter in Psalm 37:13

The psalmists sometimes rehearse the problem of the prosperity of the wicked (e.g., Ps. 73). Psalm 37 is one of the texts with many such expressions (vv. 1, 7, 12, 14, 32, 35–36), obviously a reality for David "when people succeed in their ways" (v. 7 NIV). He puts forth two solutions to the problem: be envious (v. 1) or be vindictive (v. 8); but in reality, he finds neither satisfactory. Instead of a solution, he puts forth a two-pronged resolution. The long-term approach is to recognize that the wicked's prosperity won't last forever because they will soon wither like the grass (vv. 2, 20), be destroyed (v. 9), "go up in smoke" (v. 20 NIV), and even be extinguished by their own sword (v. 15). This is the perspective the psalmist has acquired, which, admittedly, is a temporary fix. The second prong is the divine perspective, one known fully only by the Lord himself: "The Lord laughs at the wicked, *for he knows their day is coming*" (v. 13 NIV).

Over against this relentless problem, Psalm 37 commends a platform of faith and so keys us into David's own personal faith. This faith enabled his perspective on the problem: trust in the Lord (v. 3); "commit your way to the Lord" (v. 5); be still and wait patiently (v. 7); "turn away from evil and do good" (v. 27). It is indeed this program of faith that sustains the righteous and enables them to live with the persistent reality of the wicked's prosperity.

But the Lord's perspective is the tip of the pyramid, "for he knows their day is coming." God's laughter in Psalm 37, like that in Psalm 2, is the expression of his ultimate perspective on good and evil. Until that future moment in

God's redemption plan, David, and we like him, can live with the obstinate reality of injustice, as we try our hardest to fix the problem. Psalm 37:13 reduces the issue of the prosperity of the wicked to a more personal level than Psalm 2. The metaphor of the battlefield where evil combatants engage in conflict against the righteous reveals, not surprisingly, that the victims are "the poor and needy"—that is, the helpless and defenseless. The outcome is contrary to the anticipated victory of the well-weaponed warriors for evil, drawing their swords and bending their bows, ultimately to be slaughtered by their own swords. The reverberation across the combat zone was laughter, not of evil's militia—already savoring the widely expected capitulation of the hapless "poor and needy"—but of God, who had the ultimate perspective on this conflict: "The salvation of the righteous is from the LORD; he is their stronghold in the time of trouble" (37:39).

Laughter in Psalm 59:8

The third reference to God's laughter in the Psalms occurs in Psalm 59 and suggests that the lesson of Psalm 37:13 has become a standard plank in the apologetic platform of psalmic theology. Psalm 59 is David's prayer that God will deliver him from his enemies, both personal and international. For David there was not much emotional distance between the two—they all attacked him like snarling dogs looking for food. In this instance, however, the psalmist's reference to God's laughter is spoken directly to the Lord himself and, like Psalm 2, concerns the nations rather than individuals, although the nations are an extension of the personal attacks mentioned in the first part of the psalm. Moreover, the Lord's laughter at the nations, again like Psalm 2, is clearly derisive: "But you, O LORD, laugh at them; you hold all the nations in derision" (59:8). Yet, in David's mind, if the Lord is not asleep, he is definitely lethargic, and he prays that the Lord will arouse himself and take action (v. 5); and in contrast to the snarling dogs that prowl the city in the evening, David sings of the Lord's steadfast love (*hesed*) in the morning (vv. 14–16).

Concluding Remarks

God's laughter is a metaphor that illuminates the divine attributes of omniscience and omnipotence. In contrast to his earthly creatures, God has a full perspective on time and eternity, and on good and evil and their outcomes.

Further, he sometimes cannot hold back the laughter when he sees human creatures, endowed with wealth and power, waging war against the poor and needy, which is in effect warfare against God. So God laughs at their false sense of power.

When Paul and Barnabas were in Antioch in Pisidia, Paul preached a powerful sermon (Acts 13:16–41) and quoted the divine decree of Psalm 2:7: "You are my Son, today I have begotten you" (Acts 13:33). In the context of the cross and resurrection, Paul interprets "today" as the day of Christ's resurrection and the resurrection itself as the fulfillment of God's decree, "I have begotten you." The apostle makes that clear in his comment: "And we bring you the good news that what God promised to the fathers, this he has fulfilled to us their children by raising Jesus, as also it is written in the second Psalm, 'You are my Son, today I have begotten you'" (vv. 32–33). Paul probably knew Psalm 2 by heart and had the metaphor of God's laughter in mind as he recited verse 7. The psalmist's reference in Psalm 2:2 to the "kings of the earth" and "rulers" was not lost on Paul, and he identifies them in the new context of the cross and resurrection as those who put Jesus to death. They thought by this action they could obstruct God's power. But the resurrection of Jesus Christ was proof positive that humankind can never get the upper hand on God. And while the apostle does not refer specifically to God's laughter of Psalm 2:4, his use of Psalm 2:7 summons, by the interpretive method of metalepsis,[2] the whole psalm as he announces the protocols of Christ's kingdom. The echoes of God's laughter likely went through Paul's mind as they did through the psalmist's. J. S. Bach also heard the echoes as he wrote the lines to his Easter cantata in which the church joins in the joy of heaven's laughter:

> Heaven laughs! Earth rejoices,
> And all she carries in her bosom rejoices too.[3]

I sometimes wonder if we should not also break out in a holy laughter when we read the Easter message: "He is not here, for he has risen, as he said. Come, see the place where he lay" (Matt. 28:6).

---

2. On metalepsis, see note 4 in chap. 2.

3. Unger, *Handbook to Bach's Sacred Cantata Texts*, 110. "Die Himmel lacht! Die Erde jubiliereta" ("Heaven laughs, and earth rejoices") is an Easter cantata that J. S. Bach composed in Weimar in 1715 and performed on Easter Sunday, April 21, 1715.

PART 2

HUMANITY

EIGHT

The Human Condition

The Brevity of Human Life and the Certainty of Death

We are inclined to use our humanity as the lens for viewing all things. The Psalms, however, provide theological bifocals, allowing us to see our world and our lives from the divine and human perspectives. At the beginning of his *Institutes of the Christian Religion*, John Calvin says, "Nearly all the wisdom we possess, that is to say, true and sound wisdom, consists of two parts: the knowledge of God and of ourselves."[1] Even though Calvin was stating the resolve of our Christian life, not the design of the *Institutes*, the effect of his work was precisely in that direction, and his commentary on the Psalms was perhaps his most dedicated work for the achievement of that goal.

As we saw in our discussion of God's love (see chap. 2), God's love is the underlying reason for creation and the continuing thread that runs through the story of redemption. These two doctrines, creation and redemption, are merged into an inseparable relationship on the fulcrum of God's love (*hesed*).

The human condition as laid out in the Psalms is both enlightening and depressing. But that is the story of God's steadfast love in the Psalms and in Scripture generally. The Psalms often lament the brevity of life and the reality of death. Psalm 88 is the most despairing of these laments. The psalmist, who has lived his life on the edge of death (v. 15), plumbs the depths of

1. Calvin, *Institutes of the Christian Religion*, 1:35.

despondency when he laments, "Darkness is my closest friend" (Ps. 88:18 NIV):

> I call to you, LORD, every day;
>   I spread out my hands to you.
> Do you show your wonders to the dead?
>   Do their spirits rise up and praise you?
> Is your love [*hesed*] declared in the grave,
>   your faithfulness in Destruction?
> Are your wonders known in the place of darkness,
>   or your righteous deeds in the land of oblivion? (Ps. 88:9b–12 NIV)

While we may find ourselves despairing with the psalmist, we also can recognize his high view of life. As he rehearses the relationship he has had with God in life, he bemoans the fact that in death he must forfeit his life's high calling to praise God (see chap. 17, "Praise of God, the Rehearsal Hall for Eternity").

The Psalms parallel the historical books (Samuel, Kings, and Chronicles) by presenting David's life as a struggle between life and death. The forces of death were a constant threat to him: his international foes and his internal enemies—he had many of them; his love life and the tensions it produced—he was married eight times, and his children did not always have good relationships (e.g., 2 Sam. 13). Other developments troubled David, like sicknesses and diplomatic strains.

Metaphors of Mortality

The Psalms share the common theme of human mortality with the writer of Ecclesiastes, but they handle it quite differently. Certainly Psalms and Ecclesiastes share the reality of death, but the psalmists present it in more varied ways. In their language, death is generally described with vivid metaphors. Psalm 90:3–10 is one of the best examples. Human mortality is like dust, a watch in the night, a flash flood, fresh grass in the morning that withers by evening, a moan, and a bird that flies quickly away. These metaphors span the world we know and the life we live, and that is what makes them so effective. Similar descriptions of life's brevity are found in Psalms 102:3–11, 23–24 and 103:15–17 (see also Isa. 40:6–8).

Sin and Death in the Psalms

In accord with Genesis 3, the psalmists recognize the connection between sin and death. They do not retell the Genesis story, but they restate its outcomes. Sin must be viewed in that context, even though sin's story is much wider and more complicated. Most critically, sin is a "slap" in God's face because it is a violation of his character. Thankfully, God follows his own instruction, an approach that the Lord Jesus prescribes in his Sermon on the Mount: "But I say to you, Do not resist the one who is evil. But if anyone slaps you on the right cheek, turn to him the other cheek also" (Matt. 5:39). In the reality of the cross the Father turned the other cheek as his Son gave his life. For us, that "other cheek" may be a gesture of our willingness to suffer for Jesus's sake through the offense of our opponent, but for God it is forgiveness—he takes the reproach. In Isaiah's language, it is God bearing our sins for us: "But he was pierced for our transgressions; he was crushed for our iniquities; upon him was the chastisement that brought us peace, and with his wounds we are healed" (Isa. 53:5). While we may be pressed to find an equivalent to Isaiah's statement in the Psalms, the psalmists make it very clear that God is the One "who forgives all your iniquity" (Ps. 103:3), even though the gravity of our sin, assessed against the endless list of those it has offended, is beyond measure. Ultimately the Person most offended is God (51:4). When we turn the other cheek to our offenders, we are, in our own feeble way, mirroring God's absolute absorption of the sin we have committed against him, reflecting divinity's vicarious way of dealing with our sin.

The Implied Story of the Fall and Its Explicit Consequences

The Psalms, as stated above, do not tell the primordial story of the temptation and fall in Eden, but they state, restate, and lament the consequences of that story. In fact, they have their own special story to tell that bears out those consequences.

First, we should observe that the narrative of Genesis tells the story of sin and grace that the Psalms spell out in lament, praises, and meditations. The story of Cain and Abel, for example, weaves together three threads that had already begun in the story of the fall: the dissolution of social relationships; the dissolution of human-divine relationships; and the entry of death into the world. The narrative of the fall (Gen. 3) draws to a close with the detail that "the LORD God sent him [man] out from the garden of Eden to work the ground from which he was taken" (3:23). And then Cain and Abel's story begins by keying us into the detail that "Abel was a keeper of sheep, and Cain a worker of the ground" (4:2). Their occupations were an important detail of the story, for when Cain "brought to the LORD an offering of the fruit of the ground" (4:3), it reflected his audacity to present God with an offering from the ground that God had cursed. It was an "in your face" gesture, an offense to God, a "slap" in his face, so to speak. We are also informed that Abel "brought of the firstborn of his flock and of their fat portions," and "the LORD had regard for Abel and his offering, but for Cain and his offering he had no regard" (4:4–5). Obviously, our story was written not in a vacuum but out of a conscious knowledge of the sacrificial system, which used animals as sacrifices, while the fruits of the ground were secondary offerings. The result was God's favor to Abel's offering and his rejection of Cain's. And that is the first hard evidence, beyond the curses themselves (3:14–19), that humanity's ongoing story would demonstrate the dissolution of social relationships, the outcome being hatred and jealousy that resulted in Cain's murder of Abel. While this is the first acknowledgment of death in the human family, it is even more puzzling because it was fratricide. The recognition of the normal cycle of death begins in Genesis 5:5 with the announcement of Adam's death. This cycle is acknowledged in Psalm 49:10 with a reminder that all die, the fool and the wise alike, and the Levitical writer of Psalm 88 is deeply conscious that the threat of death is a lifelong burden: "Afflicted and close to death from my youth up, I suffer your terrors; I am helpless" (88:15). The fear of death was a reality, even though the psalmists do not rehearse the cause. But that is only one portion of the story. Tragically, Genesis 1–11 highlights the fact that the dissolution of human relationships is paralleled by the dissolution of the God-human relationship—God did not look with favor on Cain's offering— confirming a disruption of that fundamental relationship that had already begun in the fall (Gen. 3).

Second, the dissolution of God's plan for humanity to subdue the world (Gen. 1:28) and make it a paradise was disrupted by the human pair's disobedience, even though the tree of life was available. There are two notices of this disruption in the Genesis story, and we should observe how quickly in the story the resolution is introduced. The first comes when God saw how human wickedness had multiplied in the earth, and "the LORD regretted that he had made man on the earth, and it grieved him to his heart." While the Psalms, as we have observed, do not rehearse the Genesis story, the laments lay out in literal and metaphorical language human sin and its disastrous consequences. For example, Psalm 78:40 recalls Israel's rebellion in the wilderness, which "grieved God's heart: "So the LORD said, 'I will blot out man whom I have created from the face of the land'" (Gen. 6:6–7). By using the same verb as found in Genesis 6:6, the psalmist may intend to alert the readers concerning the gravity of Israel's sins in the wilderness, that they reached the level of the primordial sin of the human family in the Genesis story. Further, this intolerable situation was resolved, not by total destruction of the race but by the choice of one man: "But Noah found grace in the eyes of the LORD" (Gen. 6:8). That pattern would blend nicely with the closing theme of Psalm 78 that God again took drastic measures to deal with the problem by choosing the family line of Leah (Judah) over the line of Jacob's favorite wife, Rachel, to continue Israel's history. God again chose one man, David, through whom he would resolve the problem (Ps. 78:67–72).

The second phase of the dissolution/resolution narrative is related in the story of Babel with the follow-up election of Abraham. The story of the hubris of the nations is counterbalanced by the election of Abraham and God's promise that "in you all the families of the earth shall be blessed" (Gen. 12:3).

The remainder of the Old Testament is understood as the sequel to the Genesis narrative. The Levitical author of Psalm 47 sees Abraham's legacy as part of the redemptive plan: "The princes of the peoples gather as the people of the God of Abraham. For the shields of the earth belong to God; he is highly exalted!" (v. 9). As confusing as the salvation of the nations may sometimes appear in the Psalter, Psalm 87 is definitely a claim on the nations: "The LORD records as he registers the peoples, 'This one was born there'" (v. 6).

A Psalmic Sampling of the Consequences

Specifically, the dissolution of social relationships among humanity is everywhere in the Psalms. A brother turns against another brother: "You sit and speak against your brother; you slander your own mother's son" (Ps. 50:20). A close friend turns against his confidante: "For it is not an enemy who taunts me—then I could bear it; it is not an adversary who deals insolently with me—then I could hide from him. But it is you, a man, my equal, my companion, my familiar friend. We used to take sweet counsel together; within God's house we walked with the throng" (55:12–14).

Alongside the failure of social relationships, we would be justified in saying that the dissolution of the God-human relationship and the way to reverse the deterioration is one of the major topics of the Psalms. The obdurate nature of death and God's exclusive power to "redeem" one's life from death reflect the Genesis story of the fall and acknowledge God as the only hope against such a formidable power: "But God will ransom my soul from the power of Sheol, for he will receive me" (Ps. 49:15).

It would take a book and then some to rehearse the psalmic data to demonstrate this thesis fully. I am not suggesting, of course, that the psalmists were consciously trying to fill in the blanks of the Genesis story and enhance the details of sin's consequences. Yet, they lived in the theological world where those consequences had, by sheer relevance, attached themselves to the reality of human life. And that is the fundamental reason the Psalms speak so clearly to humanity.

The Brevity of Human Life and the Eternity of God

The psalmists lament the brevity of human life, and they also, reflecting the causal relationship between sin and death, lay out the disparity between the life of God and the life of humanity. The facts that God is eternal and not subject to death and that sin brought death to humanity spell out significant differences between God and humankind. There are, of course, those who would insist that "eternal" or "forever" in the Psalms and in the Old Testament generally does not mean the same as "eternal" in the New Testament. We do have to be on our intellectual toes when we read "forever" in the Psalms. Sometimes the idea of this term is merely an inestimable period of time or "in perpetuity," as in Psalm 89:1, where "to all generations" defines the term "forever": "I will sing of the steadfast love of the LORD, *forever* [*'olam*]; with my mouth I will make known your faithfulness *to all generations* [*ledor wador*, "in perpetuity"]." In other instances the expression "forever" (*'olam*) or the longer phrase that occurs at the end of the doxologies closing Psalms 41 and 106 ("Blessed be the LORD, the God of Israel, *from everlasting to everlasting* [*meha'olam we'ad ha'olam*]," 41:13; 106:48) appears to be moving more in the direction of eternity. Amos Hakham points out that each of these longer doxologies has the definite article before "forever" (*'olam* with *ha*, the definite article), and he speaks of the *'olam* of man and the *'olam* of God.[2] Whatever Hakham intends to suggest by this observation, I believe the definite article points beyond time to another reality. Referring back to a point we have made several times, the psalmists lay down a template on which the New Testament writers build their theology, which means

2. Hakham, *The Bible: Psalms*, 1:326.

there is an organic connection between the two. It is the nature of God's unfolding revelation.

Psalm 90 puts the brevity of human life (note the metaphor in v. 3) in the context of God's eternity. When Moses prays, "Teach us to number our days" (v. 12), he implies that a recognition of the brevity of life will lead to a consciousness of life's true meaning and make our earthly journey more fruitful, a fruitfulness that springs from our relationship to God, including a knowledge of God's eternal nature. Artur Weiser says the Psalms indict our sinful nature as an anesthetic agent that numbs us to the brevity of life that might otherwise diminish our love of sinning.[3] Charles Wesley struck this same note:

> Take away our love of sinning,
>   Alpha and Omega be;
> end of faith, as its beginning,
>   set our hearts at liberty.[4]

In Psalm 102, quite likely a David psalm but not labeled as such, the psalmist, probably suffering some physical affliction, describes his life "like smoke" (v. 3), and before he finishes the psalm, he declares that God will still remain after the world he created has perished. That is the writer's way of speaking about eternity, probably the closest the Psalms come to an explicit declaration that God is eternal:

> Of old you laid the foundations of the earth,
>   and the heavens are the work of your hands.
> They will perish, but you will remain;
>   they will all wear out like a garment.
> You will change them like a robe, and they will pass away,
>   but you are the same, and your years have no end. (Ps. 102:25–27)

In other words, God is not subject to the tick-tock of time that regulates our world. This statement belongs in league with the memorable declaration Moses makes in the opening of Psalm 90: "Before the mountains were brought forth, or ever you had formed the earth and the world, from everlasting to

3. Weiser, *Psalms*, 600.
4. Wesley, "Love Divine, All Loves Excelling."

everlasting you are God" (v. 2). Moses's expansive knowledge of God leads him to say that not only is God free of time's strictures, but he does not even measure time like we do. He doesn't experience the same cycle and sensation of time as human beings do: "For a thousand years in your sight are but as yesterday when it is past, or as a watch in the night" (v. 4). As the writer to the Hebrews concludes his letter, he admonishes his readers to remember their leaders and to imitate their faith, concluding with that memorable declaration of the unchanging Christ: "Jesus Christ is the same yesterday and today and forever" (Heb. 13:8). That is, Christ shares the Father's timeless being and the unique method of calculating events, and he will never change. Psalm 90 eases us along toward the declaration that God is eternal.

The Boomerang Effect of Evil

Another way the psalmists depict the relationship between sin and death is in a metaphor we might call the boomerang effect of sin. In a spiritual sense it is analogous to Newton's third law of motion: for every action there is an equal and opposite reaction. Sin creates an adverse spiritual force that recoils on itself and thus is self-destructive. This feature of moral transgression is akin to wisdom's way of describing God's relationship to his creation. The wisdom writers describe the Creator's relationship to the created order as so intimate that one can read his nature in the actions and reactions of his creation. Paul leans in this direction when he declares in Romans 1:20 that we can discern from studying the created order that there is a God: "For since the creation of the world God's invisible qualities—his eternal power and divine nature—have been clearly seen, being understood from what has been made, so that people are without excuse" (Rom. 1:20 NIV).

In the Old Testament this relationship is embodied in the law of retribution (*lex talionis*): "eye for eye, tooth for tooth, hand for hand, foot for foot, burn for burn, wound for wound, stripe for stripe" (Exod. 21:24–25). Even though *lex talionis* is not the basic law that underwrites the moral system of the Psalms, it certainly hovers over the moral system that is discernible there, and the boomerang effect of sin that is so explicit in the Psalter may be an alternate way to express *lex talionis*. That means the psalmists engage the boomerang effect to insist that the seriousness of the sin calls for a matching penalty, which is inherent in the nature of the sin itself. Or we could say with Psalm 54:5 that the boomerang nature of evil reflects the nature of God's creation. In fact, the Masoretes corrected the verb "to return/recoil" in Psalm 54:5 (*yashub* [*qal* imperfect]) to a causal reading, "to cause to return" (*yashib* [*hiphil* imperfect]), making it clear that the subject of the verb is God rather than "evil":

> Behold, <u>God</u> is my helper,
>   the Lord who supports my life.
> <u>He</u> [God] *will cause evil to recoil* (*yashib* rather than *yashub*) on my
>   slanderers;
>   in your faithfulness destroy them. (Ps. 54:4–5 AT)

Often the metaphor takes its imagery from a style of hunting. The practice of hunters was to dig a hole for a trap and then cover it with sticks and leaves. David uses this figure of speech to pray for his enemies' defeat and demise: "They dug a pit in my way, but they have fallen into it themselves" (Ps. 57:6). The figure of speech is applied to nations as well as individuals: "The nations have sunk in the pit that they made; in the net that they hid, their own foot has been caught" (Ps. 9:15; cf. 7:15).

From Human Wrath to the Praise of God

Psalm 76 employs another version of this same principle, but it falls in the fringe area of the boomerang effect of sin—that is, it is more about the sovereignty of God than about the nature of sin. At the same time, it has one of the most beautiful and hopeful statements about sin and its corollaries: "Surely the wrath of man shall praise you" (Ps. 76:10). Human actions that are intended to disarm God's sovereign movements will result in praising God rather than disqualifying him as sovereign Lord. Charles Spurgeon comments that "the wrath of man shall not only be overcome but rendered subservient to thy glory."[5] George MacDonald captures the same truth in his statement that God takes our sins as prisoners and forces them into the service of good, and "chains them like galley-slaves to the rowing-benches of the gospel-ship."[6] The question here, as with the explicit boomerang effect of sin, is whether the capability for the reversal of evil is in the nature of evil itself or in the nature of God. I would say it is in both, while divine sovereignty always takes precedence.

5. Spurgeon, *Treasury of David*, 2:304.
6. MacDonald, *Thomas Wingfold, Curate*, 596.

Psalm 64 similarly affirms God's sovereignty when the psalmist, employing one of those bold metaphors the Psalms are known for,[7] says God shoots his arrows at the psalmist's enemies (v. 7), and then he changes the subject from "God" to the understood subject, "arrows," and says: "They [the arrows] *will cause* their tongue(s) [enemies' tongues] *to stumble* on themselves" (v. 8 AT). In effect, "God" of verse 7 is the implied agent of verse 8, even though the explicit subject is "arrows": God is the one who shoots them. While the Hebrew grammar is a bit muddled, the sense of God's sovereign actions is clear.

The psalmists clearly employ the boomerang effect of evil without trying to prove it; like wisdom writers, they simply take it as a theological given. We could construct a list of citations from our own world that would also affirm this principle. The bottom line is that it is the sovereign God who controls all things. The absolutism of this statement may make us feel uncomfortable in a world where evil is rampant and so often seems to overpower good. Yet, the topic of this chapter opens a window into how the psalmists view the power of evil and its quality of self-destruction, while at the same time affirming the truth that God is sovereign. When all the data are in, God is the controlling explanation for everything.

---

7. See "Bold Metaphors and Their Truth Value" in chap. 7.

NINE

We Become Like Our God

The "Image of God": Its Offensive and Defensive Functions

One of the most wonderful concepts in the Bible, yet one of the most mysterious, is the creation of humanity in God's image (Gen. 1:26). The creation of humankind in the image of God can be viewed, to use a sports metaphor, as having an offensive and defensive side. Offensively, the image of God is the magnificent act of grace, the beginning of the arc of redemption that connects to the glorious re-creation of humanity in the image of Christ. It shows how special humanity is to God, that he would create them in his own image. Defensively, the image of God puts these special creatures at a proper distance from God, a reminder that they are not God, for they are created *in* God's image. Christ is the real image of God, into which God will transform us. That does not mean we will become "little Christs," but we will be remade in Christ's likeness. The preposition of the phrase "*in* the image of God" (1:27) is both a connector and a separator.

As previously noted, the phrase "image of God" does not appear in Scripture again after the Noah story (Gen. 9:6), but the wonder and mystery of humankind created in the image of God are threaded throughout the Old Testament. John Calvin says that the inevitable sequel of humanity's sinful nature is that God re-creates humans in *his* image, or humankind creates God in *their* image.[1] This is the crux of the biblical story, with idolatry the

---

1. Selderhuis (*Calvin's Theology of the Psalms*, 45) draws this point from Calvin's discussion of Ps. 100:1 in his *Commentary on the Book of Psalms*.

result of the latter transaction (humankind creates God in *their* image) and redemption the cure. The biblical story begins with God's endowment of his image to humankind and all that follows discloses in varying degrees the divine initiative and the human response.

The genealogy of Genesis 5 gives the impression that this paradigm is already in the mind of our narrator. First, the narrator uses different verbs to distinguish God's creative activity from Adam's procreative activity—God *creates,* humankind *procreates.* The verb "to create" (*br'*) describes God's activity, while the verb "to beget" (*hiphil* of *yld,* "to give birth") describes Adam's activity ("fathered," vv. 3–4). The result highlights the difference between God's capability to create humankind in his own image and humanity's procreative ability to produce offspring in their own image.

Second, it is interesting, and I think significant, that both phrases from Genesis 1:26, "in our image, after our likeness" (*betsalmenu kidmutenu*), appear in 5:3, although they are interchanged ("in his likeness, after his image"). This switching of the two terms may be the author's subtle way to get our attention: he wants us to note that this was Adam's endowment of the human image to his offspring, whereas in Genesis 1:26 it was God's endowment of the divine image to his creation. The point of the text is to highlight that difference: "This is the story of Adam's family. When God *created* [*br'*] mankind, *he created* [*br'*] him *in the likeness of God* [*bidmut 'elohim*], male and female *he created* [*br'*] them, and he called their name mankind when *he created* [*br'*] them. And when Adam had lived 130 years, *he begot* [*yoled*] *in his likeness* [*badmuto*], *according to his own image* [*ketsalmo*], and he called his name Seth" (Gen. 5:1–3 AT).[2]

EXCURSUS: PSALM 8 AND THE IMAGE OF GOD

The book of Genesis paints a picture of the landscape of the biblical story with a broad brush, including creation, the patriarchs, and the covenants. Genesis also incorporates some of the key terms of divine revelation—for example, the image of God—which is not coincidental. Even though the phrase does not occur again in the Bible after Genesis 9, Psalm 8 introduces its own beautiful way of referring to

2. The clause "he begot in his likeness, according to his own image" does not have a direct object in the Hebrew (even though many English translations supply "son" as the object). Rather, the phrase "in his likeness, according to his own image" functions as an adverbial phrase, suggesting that the emphasis falls on the verb "begot," and the adverbial phrase modifies the verb ("how" or "in what manner").

that truth, "a little lower than God" (AT), and the wonder of the human creation as laid out in Scripture, especially in the Psalms, is a commentary on that phrase.

In the context of God's awesome creation of the world the psalmist asks the ontological question: "What is man that you are mindful of him, and the son of man that you care for him?" (Ps. 8:4). The supplicant hints at the source of his wonderment—that is, "the image of God"—when he recalls the elevated status of humankind's creation: "You have made him a little lower than God and crowned him with glory and honor" (v. 5 AT).[3] Then the psalmist unfolds the coordinate function of humanity that was appropriate to their exalted status: "You have given him dominion over the works of your hand; you have put all things under his feet, all sheep and oxen, and also the beasts of the field, the birds of the heavens, and the fish of the sea, whatever passes along the paths of the seas" (vv. 6–8). In other words, it was not enough for God to create human beings in the elevated status of "a little lower than God," but he assigned responsibilities to his most noble creatures that were appropriate for the status.

Original Sin as Idolatry: Genesis 3

Scripture's depth of understanding human creatures and their natural inclinations is beyond awesome. Genesis 3 tells the story of how God's highest creation decided to project themselves into a position infinitely beyond their capabilities, indeed, into godlike beings. The serpent's scheme drew upon that innate desire to be like God, planted in humans by the very nature of their creation in God's image. And who with the mysterious and marvelous nature of humanity would not want to become like the Creator!

So the serpent taps into that longing but with a malicious twist, turning the first couple's legitimate desire into a false claim of godlikeness: "For God knows that when you eat of it your eyes will be opened, and you will be like God, knowing good and evil" (Gen. 3:5). The woman even surveys the tree with perceptive discernment and sees that its fruit offers the ingredients for the ideal life: "So when the woman saw that the tree was good for food, and that it was a delight to the eyes, and that the tree was to be desired to make one wise . . ." (v. 6).[4] The first couple has their eyes on the right goal, to become

---

3. See discussion about this translation under "The Language of Creation" in chap. 1.

4. John seems to express these three qualities in their transmuted form: "For all that is in the world—the desires of the flesh and the desires of the eyes and pride of life—is not from the Father but is from the world" (1 John 2:16).

like God, but they take the wrong path to reach it: disobedience of God's command. God's command was a microcosm of the larger plan revealed in the Bible that demands fidelity to the Creator. The eye-opening outcome of their act is a revelation of their nature now transmuted by their choice of disobedience: "they knew that they were naked. And they sewed fig leaves together and made themselves loincloths" (v. 7). It is idolatry in its incipient and most flagrant form, a projection of the human self into a god. The fall of humanity was in the act of trying to become God, rather than become *like* God.

The Creator's response is to find where they are hiding: "Where are you?" (Gen. 3:9). C. S. Lewis remarks that Christianity is the only religion which holds that God takes the initiative, that he comes seeking us human beings. Although there is some truth to the idea that humanity must look for God, the primary issue is who takes the initiative. Christianity holds that God does. God comes looking for us before we have even thought about looking for him. Paul says, "But God shows his love for us in that *while we were still sinners*, Christ died for us" (Rom. 5:8).

A Paradigm of Redemption's Story (Gen. 1–3)

As the beginning of the story of redemption, Genesis 1–3 is also a parable of the relationship between God and humanity in salvation history: humanity hides from God, and God seeks humanity. While we can view the story as an isolated account, it is nevertheless a microcosmic representation of the larger plan of redemption, a paradigm of redemption in which the Creator seeks his offending and hiding creatures. And not surprisingly, the blame game begins:

The Lord God: "Where are you?"

The man: "I was afraid, because I was naked, and I hid myself."

The Lord God: "Who told you that you were naked? Have you eaten of the tree of which I commanded you not to eat?"

The man: "The woman whom you gave to be with me, she gave me fruit of the tree, and I ate."

The Lord God to the woman: "What is this that you have done?"

The woman: "The serpent deceived me, and I ate." (Gen. 3:9–13)

The Lord God's response begins at the root of the problem, pronouncing curses on the offenders in the order of their actions: first, the serpent, who introduces the issue; second, the woman, who initiates the human response; and third, the man, who follows the woman's lead:

The Lord God to the serpent:

> "Because you have done this,
>   cursed are you. . . .
> I will put enmity between you and the woman,
>   and between your offspring and her offspring;
> he shall bruise your head,
>   and you shall bruise his heel."

The Lord God to the woman:

> "I will surely multiply your pain in childbearing;
>   in pain you shall bring forth children.
> Your desire shall be contrary to your husband,
>   but he shall rule over you."

The Lord God to the man:

> "Because you have listened to the voice of your wife
>   and have eaten of the tree
> of which I commanded you,
>   'You shall not eat of it,'
> cursed is the ground because of you;
>   in pain you shall eat of it all the days of your life. . . ."

The story continues:

> And the LORD God made for Adam and for his wife garments of skins and clothed them.
>   Then the LORD God said, "Behold, the man has *become like one of us* in knowing good and evil. Now, lest he reach out his hand and take also of the tree of life and eat, and live forever—" therefore the LORD God sent him out from the garden of Eden to work the ground from which he was taken. He drove out the man, and at the east of the garden of Eden he placed the cherubim and a flaming sword that turned every way to guard the way to the tree of life. (Gen. 3:14–24)

At this point, the story of redemption—a trace of which already appears in the curse of the woman, "he shall bruise your head, and you shall bruise his heel" (3:15)—begins to unfold. It stretches the length of Holy Scripture, in varying degrees from book to book. It is also significant to note that the name of the deity, "God" (*'elohim*) in Genesis 1 and "Lord God" (*Yahweh 'elohim*) in Genesis 2–3, is a worthy theological distinction in the narrative. As the rabbis remind us, when the name of the deity is "God" (*'elohim*), the implication is the God of power, and when it is "Lord" (*Yahweh*), it signifies the God of mercy and grace (see Exod. 34:6–7).[5]

We should note that the organization of these opening chapters of Genesis validates this interpretation. It is only in the second story of creation (Gen. 2:4–25) and the companion story of the fall (Gen. 3) that we are, by the addition of the name Lord/Yahweh, introduced to the profile of the God of power *and* grace. Furthermore, the hands-on version of creation in Genesis 2 reveals to us the nature of God as a personal God; he not only creates man and woman with his own hands but enters into a relationship with them. And that sets the stage for understanding the God of Scripture: he is a personal God. Thus the opening chapters of Genesis, by design, give us complementary portraits of God: the transcendent God (Gen. 1) and the immanent God (Gen. 2–3). The rest of Scripture unfolds these complementary portraits, which are one and the same (see also "The Oratorio of Creation and Redemption (Ps. 19)" in chap. 1).

The point of this discussion, which may at first seem to be a diversion, is that the forward-moving thrust of redemption is anchored in God's endowment of humanity with his own image, coupled with revelatory hints of his redeeming plan in Genesis 2–3. The first couple's desire to be like God was legitimate, but by the serpent's twisted logic and their own self-aggrandizing choice, they took the wrong path to the goal. And this is the path on which idolatry waits for every unsuspecting recruit.

The Position of Psalms 115:2–8 and 135:13–18 in Book 5

The psalmist's insightful statement of the principle of idolatry is, "Those who make them become like them; so do all who trust in them" (115:8; 135:18). The content of these duplicate denunciations is of theological significance, enhanced by their position in Book 5.

5. The source critics have emphasized the priestly literary source (P) as the basis for Gen. 1–3. While the idea of literary/theological sources in Genesis is a given, I think the literary source critics have sometimes failed to recognize the theological distinctions of the sources and as a result have missed the author's/editor's theological thrust.

The first occurrence is in the group of psalms called the Egyptian Hallel (Pss. 113–18), which became a liturgy for the Jewish Passover. In their psalmic settings, Psalms 115 and 135 are strategically placed so that the Egyptian Hallel—celebrating the first exodus from Egypt (Ps. 114) as the model for the second exodus from Babylonian exile (Ps. 113),[6] culminating with the rebuilding of the temple (Ps. 118)—is a statement of the new community's identity.[7] A centerpiece of the Hallel was the polemic against idolatry in 115:2–8, which amounted to a rejection of idolatry by the postexilic community. The magnitude of idolatry, in the view of Ezekiel, himself a prophet in exile, can be seen in that prophet's assertion that the exile was Israel's punishment for idolatry (Ezek. 36:16–18; implied in 14:11 and 37:23).

In Psalm 115 the denunciation of idolatry is the response to the nations' taunting question: "Where is their God?" The short answer is: "Our God is in the heavens; he does all that he pleases" (vv. 2–3), and then follows the description:

> Their idols are silver and gold,
> > the work of human hands.
> They have mouths, but do not speak;
> > eyes, but do not see.
> They have ears, but do not hear;
> > noses, but do not smell.
> They have hands, but do not feel;
> > feet, but do not walk;
> > and they do not make a sound in their throat.
> Those who make them become like them;
> > so do all who trust in them. (Ps. 115:4–8)

Our God who is in the heavens is also the God who made the heavens and the earth (115:15); he is therefore the God of life, not death, as the lifeless idols symbolize—they have no sign of life, and those who make them become like them (v. 8). The idol worshipers are spiritually dead like their gods, and "the

---

6. In Ps. 113 the psalmist uses the metaphor of a "barren" woman to describe the country in exile and quotes from the Song of Hannah (113:8 quotes 1 Sam. 2:8a–c). In ancient Israel barrenness was a humiliation. This metaphor was perfect for the exile, which the poet describes as "the refuse dump": "He raises the weak/poor from the dust; he elevates the needy from the refuse dump, to make [them] sit with princes" (Ps. 113:7–8a AT//1 Sam. 2:8a–c). See Bullock, *Psalms*, 2:315–16, 318.

7. See Bullock, "The Egyptian Hallel (Psalms 113–18)," in *Psalms*, 2:322–23.

dead do not praise the LORD, nor do any who go down into silence" (v. 17). That puts the true believers who worship the true God in the category of the God of life, and "we will bless the LORD from this time forth and for evermore. Praise the LORD!" (v. 18).

The second denunciation in Psalm 135:15–18, a virtual duplicate of 115:4–8, occurs after the Songs of Ascent (Pss. 120–34). It forms the last stanza of the psalm, before its concluding word of praise (135:19–21; cf. 115:9–11). This denunciation is not a response to a question as in Psalm 115, but it invokes the memory of Moses and the plagues on Egypt (135:8–9) and the conquest of Canaan (135:10–12). Like the burning bush incident (Exod. 3:15), Psalm 135 engages Yahweh's name and his ability to "vindicate his people and have compassion on his servants" (135:14), just like he did in Egypt and the wilderness. The "Name" theology is prominent in this psalm, the divine name, Yahweh (*YHWH*, "LORD"), occurring 18 times in the psalm. The opening stanza of Psalm 135 is, not surprisingly, an extended call to praise the Lord, and we might consider Psalm 136 as the fulfillment of that summons. It is my contention that the polemic against idolatry in Psalms 115 and 135 is not causal but constitutes a repudiation of idolatry, reflecting the postexilic community's decision to acknowledge and worship Yahweh alone. At the grassroots level in Israel's preexilic history, they were a henotheistic rather than a monotheistic people, acknowledging Yahweh as their God but not denying that other gods existed.[8] The exile purged them of that fallacy.

The Fatal Product of Idolatry

The polemic against idolatry in Psalms 115:4–8 and 135:15–18 is very broad, involving both the makers *and* the worshipers of idols, the whole gamut, and the end product is the same: both the makers and worshipers "become like them." The significant feature of the description is that the idols are made out of the finest of metals—silver and gold—and in the form of their human creators, but their sensory organs are nonetheless dysfunctional. They have mouths but cannot speak, eyes but cannot see, ears but cannot hear, noses but cannot smell, hands but cannot feel, throats but cannot utter a sound. Their makers and worshipers alike have projected themselves onto their gods, who are lifeless—they can do nothing. In contrast, the Lord, Maker of heaven

---

8. See Bullock, "Yahweh and Other Gods in the Psalter," in *Psalms*, 1:54.

and earth (115:15), "does all that he pleases" (v. 3). This latter clause is not a statement of God's freedom to do whatever he wants to do, operating without ethical constraints; rather, it reflects God's freedom to act, his capability to act, out of his character. The primary emphasis falls on the verb "does" ('asah), in contrast to the idols who can *do nothing*. While they can do nothing, Yahweh is the Creator of heaven and earth, an ability of epic proportions. If the idols, by human estimation, have a sterling character, made of silver and gold, but have no capability to act, that helplessness puts them in a totally different category than the Lord, who made heaven and earth. Moreover, the Lord is a personal God who can relate to humans because they possess his sensory capabilities, expressing their personal nature. But the idols are deficient in all the sensory capabilities that God, Maker of heaven and earth, used in the work of creation:

Mouth—God *spoke* and the world came into existence.

Eyes—God *saw* his works and called them good.

Ears—God *heard* Adam and Eve speaking.

Nose—God *breathed* the breath of life into man's nostrils.

Hands—God *formed* man from the dust of the ground.

Feet—God *walked* in the garden.

Throat—God not only could speak but could issue oracles of blessing and judgment.

The idols had none of these capabilities. They were a projection of their makers into the place of God, repeating the sin of Adam and Eve, whom the serpent tempted with the promise "you will be like God" (Gen. 3:5), which the Lord God himself conceded: "The man has become *like one of us* in knowing good and evil" (3:22). But the end result was precisely what the Lord God had said: they would die (3:3), and indeed they did (5:5). Significantly, this contradicted the serpent's promise, "You will not surely die" (3:4). While the serpent had been partly right ("your eyes will be opened, and you will be like God, knowing good and evil"; 3:4–5), he said nothing about the insubordination into which his suggestion would thrust the human pair. Further, part of the subtlety of the serpent's strategy was to add truth to falsehood, a mode of argument that tragically became timeless and devastating to truth.

The couple's action had two outcomes. The first was death. Adam's death did not occur until he and Eve had carried out the mandate to populate the earth (Gen. 5:5). Yet, by their disobedience they had mapped out the path to death for all idolators: "The dead do not praise the LORD, nor do any who go down into silence [death]. But we will bless the LORD from this time forth and forevermore. Praise the LORD!" (Ps. 115:17–18).

The second outcome was the knowledge of good and evil, first introduced in company with the tree of life in Genesis 2:9 without any explanatory note. The following mention of the tree of the knowledge of good and evil in 2:16–17 is paired with the Lord God's mandate forbidding Adam to eat of the tree of the knowledge of good and evil. The third occurrence of the phrase in Genesis 3:5 is prompted and crafted by the serpent. Imputing the reference to God, the serpent denies that death will be the penalty for partaking of the tree. This devious creature is certainly correct to say the knowledge of God is a godlike trait ("You will be like God," Gen. 3:5), and the serpent's plan is already in place in his scheming mind. Yet, the fact that God does not attach an explanatory note to the mandate is still a quandary. Of note is that any sense of obedient trust between God and his human creatures was obliterated: "Now, lest he reach out his hand and take also of the tree of life and eat, and live forever . . . " (Gen. 3:22). The tree of life had not been explicitly forbidden to them, and the implied story is that they could have procured eternal life, or some distorted version of it, along the same forbidden path they had chosen: "therefore the LORD God sent him out from the garden of Eden to work the ground from which he was taken" (v. 23). The human destiny, intended to be from earth to eternal life, was now from earth to earth. And that tragic dilemma, facilitated by death, was the inescapable impasse that faced humanity from that point forward to the promise of the resurrection to eternal life through Jesus Christ. Using the argument of *qal vahomer* Paul presents this truth in the redemptive frame of Christ's death and resurrection: "For if, because of one man's trespass, death reigned through that one man, much more will those who receive the abundance of grace and the free gift of righteousness reign in life through the one man Jesus Christ" (Rom. 5:17).

The makers and worshipers, like their idols, became mute, blind, and deaf. That is, they had become lifeless. It is quite significant that when the writer of Psalm 135 picks up the polemic from 115:4–8, he beautifully expands the call to praise, summoning all Israel and all God-fearers to praise the Lord (135:19–21). Without saying so, our poet finds a solace in the praise of God, who "does what he pleases" (135:8), and God's people know what pleases him because they have read his gracious character (135:14) by bringing them out of the bondage of Egypt and through the unpredictable dangers of the wilderness (135:8–14). With that as their grateful heritage, another servant of God in another era pondered in elation, "What no eye has seen, nor ear heard, nor the heart of man imagined, what God has prepared for those who love him" (1 Cor. 2:9).

Other Biblical Warrants

The Torah has its own distinct way of articulating the principle set forth in Psalm 115:8. The Lord says, "Be holy, for I am holy" (Lev. 11:44). That is, be like your God; replicate his character. Greg Beale, in his excellent and thorough study of this theological principle, demonstrates how numerous Old Testament texts convey the same message, including Jeremiah 2:5 and 2 Kings 17:15.[9] The prophet Jeremiah proclaimed that message to Jerusalem, agreeing with Ezekiel that idolatry was Israel's pivotal sin:

This is what the LORD says:

"What fault did your ancestors find in me,
    that they strayed so far from me?
They followed worthless idols
    and became worthless themselves." (Jer. 2:5 NIV)

This is the precise message of Psalms 115 and 135—the makers and worshipers of idols "become like them." In describing Israel's (the Northern Kingdom's) exile to Assyria, the writer of Kings also explains that Israel refused to obey the torah that the Lord had commanded them through his servants the prophets and became idolaters: "But they would not listen and were as stiff-necked as their ancestors, who did not trust in the LORD their God. They rejected his decrees and the covenant he had made with their ancestors and the statutes he had warned them to keep. *They followed worthless idols and themselves became worthless*" (2 Kings 17:14–15 NIV). In view of the wide distribution of this theme in the Old Testament, as Beale demonstrates, and the "sensory-organ-malfunction language"[10] that describes the malfunction

9. Beale, *We Become What We Worship*, 70–126.
10. Beale, *We Become What We Worship*, 41.

of the organs of spiritual perception, we can conclude that the first sin of Genesis 3 was also idolatry and, dare we say it, our sin when we make and worship our idols, whatever form they take. Idolatry was a repetition of the original sin, and all Israel, some coming out of the Babylonian exile of suffering and humiliation, joined in a hymn of summative praise to the God of all gods.

Creation and Re-creation: Becoming the Image of Christ

The importance of creation in the Bible cannot be exaggerated. Paul uses the model of creation to speak about redemption, and very often these two fundamental doctrines of Scripture are brought together in the Psalms (see chap. 1, "The *Aleph* and *Tav* of Psalmic Theology"). In 2 Corinthians Paul connects the "light of the gospel that displays the glory of Christ, who is the image of God," to the Creator God, who said, "Let light shine out of darkness," the same God who "made light shine in our hearts to give us the light of the knowledge of God's glory displayed in the face of Christ" (2 Cor. 4:4–6 NIV). The light that illuminated the world in creation is connected—indeed lights up the world again in all its glory—with the face of Jesus Christ. In Colossians 3:10 the apostle describes the transformative power of redemption as "put[ting] on the new self, which is being renewed in knowledge after *the image of its creator*." Paul's argument is that the power of redeeming grace transforms us or, we may say, re-creates us in the "image of God" by making us into the "image of Christ"; in his Corinthian correspondence the terms are synonymous. In Romans 8:29 Paul says the object of redemption is that we may be "conformed to the image of his Son."

We in our fallen nature are prone to project ourselves into God's place, like Adam and Eve did. The woman recognized the tree's God-endowed nature, that it "was good for food, and that it was a delight to the eyes, and that the tree was to be desired to make one wise" (Gen. 3:7)—all three traits essential to fulfilled humanity. The human desire, exacerbated by the serpent, induced the craving to partake. The story leaves the impression that the tree was not misrepresented—it did represent the potential to know good and evil (3:5), a trait that, we are informed later (3:5), characterizes God. Rather, the human couple's violation consisted of disobeying God's command not to eat of the tree (2:16–17; 3:3). In fact, the apostle John acknowledges that the outcome of seeing God is not death, as it was in the Old Testament, but becoming like God: "Dear friends, now we are children of God, and what we will be has not yet been made known. But we know that when Christ appears, we shall be like him, for we shall see him as he is" (1 John 3:2 NIV).

Paul then teaches that the objective of redeeming grace is conforming us to the image of Christ, who is "the image of God." So in redemption God returns to the original creation of humankind in the image of God and *re-creates* them *in the image of Christ*, who is God in human flesh—oh, the wonder and the mystery! We cannot enter here into the theological argument regarding whether the image of God was obliterated or just marred by the fall. The argument is essentially contingent upon how we define the image of God, and I would insist that it includes the spiritual, rational, and even the physical aspects in the "incarnational" sense of the word. That is, when God chose to reveal himself to the fullest extent, he chose to do it by becoming human. Some would hesitate to include the physical nature of humanity as endemic to the image of God, but the person of God is clearly presented in Scripture as possessing all of those faculties, even though we often call the physical descriptions of God "anthropomorphisms" and might also name the spiritual and rational aspects "anthropopathisms." By any measurement of standards, however, the fact that these attributes are absolutely conducive to our understanding of God and God's nature means that he is a personal God. In Christian theology we revel in the fact that God chose the human form and aptitudes to impart the pinnacle of his self-revelation in Jesus of Nazareth, born of Mary. In the Lord Jesus's exchange with Philip in John 14 he says, "Have I been with you so long, and you still do not know me, Philip? Whoever has seen me has seen the Father" (John 14:9).

When Scripture speaks of God's redeeming work of grace, creation is not far behind. Quite beautifully does Jesus articulate the final chapter of redemption in the language of creation: "Behold, I make all things new" (Rev. 21:5 KJV).

A Timeless Warning for Idolators

We by our fallen nature are inclined to project ourselves into God's place of honor and power, so we sometimes mindlessly look for symbols of honor and power, and they become our idols—sometimes even before we become conscious of our sinful replacement syndrome. While the Psalms do not inveigh against idolatry as strongly as the prophets do, the polemic in Psalms 115 and 135 is an assessment of the end product of idol worship that ought to alert us to our obsession for power and honor and many other things, things that will make us into facsimiles of what we idolize, only to speed us down the road to believing they are the real thing. Then and there we have become like our idols: mute, blind, deaf, and lifeless.

The worship of lifeless idols, whatever form it takes, is a hint of the helplessness and hopelessness of idolatry, humanity's first sin. Isaiah paints a stunning picture of the human dilemma when the idols that humans make and worship are put to the test. Deficient of normal human capabilities, they have to be carried on beasts of burden, even though they are supposed to carry their worshipers to safety in their desperation; then they are carried off into captivity:

> Bel bows down; Nebo stoops;
> > their idols are on beasts and livestock;
> these things you carry are borne
> > as burdens on weary beasts.
> They stoop; they bow down together;
> > they cannot save the burden,
> > but themselves go into captivity. (Isa. 46:1–2)

In contrast, our God, our Maker, is the only One capable of saving us from our self-created and self-imposed impasses of life: "I have made you and I will carry you; I will sustain you and I will rescue you" (Isa. 46:4 NIV). Creation ("I have made you") presupposes redemption ("and I will carry you"). The story of redemption is about God's reclaiming the world he made, reclaiming it from the false claims that his human creatures made in Adam and Eve and their countless successive generations. It is the spirit that took hold of Adam and Eve in the garden and removed the possessive pronoun "yours" that pronounced the world God's, scrawling over it the pronoun "mine" instead. That pronoun was written in elongated script, in the self-aggrandizing spirit of the creatures. But the story of reclamation is the story of the cross and the resurrection. Our children's kindergarten teacher, a raconteur of merit, told the story of a little boy who entered her class before Christmas one year and heard her tell the story of Christmas. He was so impressed and touched by it that he spoke to a fellow student about his feelings, and this little guy said to him, "If you think the Christmas story is great, just wait till you hear the Easter story!"

Our God, truly and thankfully, carries forth his re-creating work to conform the damaged image of God to the new and perfect image of Christ. The work begun along the path of disobedience is finally accomplished by the re-creating work of our obedient Christ, and as God intended from the foundation of the world, we become like our God. That's the story of redemption and hopefully the story of our Christian life.

TEN

Shamed and Shaming

Shame is a topic often engaged by the psalmists. Its frequency in the Psalms reveals the critical part this emotion played in the life of the ancients. Its breadth in the Psalter is wide, ranging from an international concern that the nations be ashamed of their ungodly ways (Ps. 83:17), to David's very personal prayer that Yahweh would not let "those who hope in you be put to shame through me, O Lord GOD of hosts; let not those who seek you be brought to dishonor through me, O God of Israel" (69:6). Moreover, the linguistic range of "shame" in the Psalms is quite extensive, involving at least seven different verbs and many nouns.[1] In a world, particularly the Western world, where shame has virtually been disqualified as having any constructive value, this topic, so frequently voiced in the Psalms, deserves a renewed awareness and a revival of conscience.

Shame and Guilt Compared

Generally speaking, shame is demeaning. It makes us feel worthless and collapses our ego. Its negative effect can become a spiritual and psychological burden. Lyn M. Bechtel has done a commendable study on shame as a sanction of social control in the biblical world and makes a convincing case for shame as a more powerful force than guilt.[2] This is most likely because the

1. See this linguistic range in Bechtel, "Shame as a Sanction of Social Control in Biblical Israel," 54–55.
2. Bechtel, "Shame as a Sanction of Social Control in Biblical Israel," 55, 76.

effect of shame is more enduring than guilt, laying a pall of humiliation on an individual and his or her family and clan, often for generations. In the book of Ruth, when the primary redeemer hears that redeeming the property of Naomi's sons carries the obligation to marry Naomi's widowed daughter-in-law Ruth, he declines the "honor," only to bear the disreputable name "The Family of the Unsandaled" (Deut. 25:10 NIV; cf. Ruth 4:7). The name itself implies that the shame is not merely a personal matter for the would-be redeemer but the family shares the shame.[3]

Guilt, on the other hand, is punishment-directed. Once the punishment is implemented, the matter is, for the most part, concluded; the shame associated with the crime does not necessarily continue to apply. The debt has been paid. The biblical world was much more group oriented than our individualistic Western world. Even the principle espoused by Ezekiel—as wonderful as it was—that a person will not suffer for one's parents' sins but only for one's own (Ezek. 18) does not implicitly endorse the kind of individualism developed in the modern world. The social implications of our extreme individualism involve the decline and even the demise of shame because social entities have lost their coherence. Many families, for example, do not take care of their parents and grandparents in old age. Often families are divided by geographical distance, political association, and other dynamics. Shaming as a social sanction to control behavior and protect family and group reputations has lost its power.

But that is only one side of the coin. The other side is that morality, especially of the Judeo-Christian persuasion, has long been in decline. This decline and the loss of social cohesiveness in the West together share much of the culpability for the regression of shame as a moral force in our world. As we will note below, there are social and theological implications for this development.

EXCURSUS: AN ANALOGY FOR THE EDITING PROCESS OF THE PSALMS

Even though the topic of this excursus may seem to be a diversion, it is necessary to understand how the Psalter has been composed. The book of Psalms is the result of a long editing process over several centuries. While this process is not what we might expect today, the analogy of a palimpsest manuscript may help us

3. See the excursus "Boaz the 'Redeemer' (Go'el)" in chap. 1.

understand it better. A palimpsest is a manuscript that a later scribe has erased and reused for a new document. We can immediately recognize the challenges this practice would create, since the underlying script was sometimes still visible.[4]

The editorial process was a complex undertaking. It involved, for example, small collections of psalms placed at strategic points in the collection, like the Korah psalms (Pss. 42–49, 84–85, 87–88) and the Asaph Psalms (Pss. 50, 73–83), and of course the David psalms that are distributed throughout the five books of the Psalter.[5] When the editors undertook their task, performed intermittently over a long period of time, they did not take the book apart and start all over. Rather they reworked the collections at hand, and when we examine our present Psalter, we can frequently see signs of that process.

This is the case with Psalm 70, which is a duplicate of Psalm 40:13–17. The editor of Book 2 (Pss. 42–72), working with the Davidic character of Book 1 (Pss. 1–41), crafted the closing of Book 2 (particularly Pss. 69–71) to reflect David's concerns in Book 1 (particularly Ps. 40:13–17) and engaged three webbing themes from Psalm 40. What the editor intended to do was to make a logical and smooth transition from Book 2 to Book 3 (Pss. 73–89), while ending Book 2 in a way that corresponds closely to the Davidic ending of Book 1 in Psalms 40–41.

Repetition was an effective composition technique in the ancient world. The editorial process therefore involved repetition of already used materials and the insertion of new materials— such as "author" collections mentioned above—and "type" collections (e.g., the *maskil* psalms [Pss. 52–55] and the *miktam* psalms [Pss. 56–60]). Thus the editorial process involved enhancements to the collection already at hand. This also reminds us of the four concluding doxologies, the editorial feature that came at some point in the process to conclude the first four books of the Psalter. Their addition was likely at a stage of the compositional history when the editors wanted to give each book some stability and closure and when the general thrust of the collection had already taken on the tenor of praise, since these four benedictions are directed toward that end (each begins "Blessed be the Lord, God of Israel"). Judging from the fact that these doxologies already appear in the Septuagint (second century BC), they were likely quite early. This does not mean that each book was forever closed. Later editors took advantage of editorial changes that presented themselves.

It should be further noted that the final collection of David psalms in Book 5 (Pss. 138–45) left a note to remind the readers that the writer was aware of the formal doxologies that conclude Books 1–4, preserving two linguistic characteristics

4. With modern technology we can sometimes read the underlying script as well as the script imposed on it.

5. The David psalms: Book 1, Pss. 3–41; Book 2, Pss. 51–65, 68–70; Book 3, Ps. 86; Book 4, Pss. 101, 103; Book 5, Pss. 108–10, 122, 124, 131, 138–45.

of those four doxologies: the verb "bless" (*brk*) and the noun/adverb "forever" (*'olam*): "My mouth will speak of the praise of the LORD. May all flesh *bless* his holy name *forever* and ever" (Ps. 145:21; also v. 1; AT). The final collection was then concluded with a set of praise psalms, a crescendo of praise (Pss. 146–50).

Three Webbing Themes Picked Up from Psalm 40

David's Enemies

The themes of Psalm 40 are picked up in Psalms 69, 70, and 71, as Book 2 transitions to Book 3. They are laid out in a way that I have called "webbing" themes. The editor wants the readers to see the relationship to Psalm 40. The first webbing theme picked up from Psalm 40 (see the excursus "An Analogy for the Editing Process of the Psalms" above) is the topic of David's enemies (Ps. 40:13, 17), which dominates Book 1 and is found in the psalms transitioning from Book 2 to Book 3 (Pss. 69:4, 7, 9–39; 70:1–3; and 71:4, 9–13). Not surprisingly, this is also a major topic when the writer of the book of Samuel reflects on David's life. In fact, the writer positions this landmark note in 2 Samuel 7:1: "After David was settled in his palace and *the* LORD *had given him rest from all his enemies around him*"; and then he appends the statement, "he [David] said to Nathan the prophet, 'Here I am, living in a house of cedar, while the ark of God remains in a tent'" (7:2). This comment follows the record of 2 Samuel 6, another landmark annotation, that David had moved the ark to Jerusalem; now with the cessation of military activities noted in 2 Samuel 7, King David can finally leverage his attention to building the temple. Moreover, Psalm 69:9 drops a clue about the opposition that David's passion for building the temple created: "For zeal for your house has consumed me, and the reproaches of those who reproach you have fallen on me" (see the discussion below).

David's Urgent Plea That the Lord "Hurry" and Act

The second webbing theme picked up from Psalm 40 is the plea that God would act hurriedly (40:13, 17//Pss. 69:17; 70:1, 5). To understand this urgency, we have to recognize that, as Book 2 transitions to Book 3, the editor of Book 3 is evidently aware of the destruction of the temple and Babylonian exile that form the historical backdrop for Book 3 (see Pss. 74:1–11, 22–23; 79:11–13).

In that time of uncertainty and humiliation, divine haste was imperative. The absence of the temple and the threat of Israel's disappearance as a people, generated by the exile, made the moment strategically urgent.

David's Prayer That He Will Never Be Put to Shame

The third webbing theme picked up from Psalm 40 is the topic of shame (40:14–15; 69:6–7; 70:2–3; 71:1, 13, 24). This particular topic stands at the center of David's words on shame in the pericope of Psalms 69–71 that facilitates the transition to Book 3.[6] Psalm 69 is a lament, and David confesses at the beginning that he is almost drowning in trouble generated by countless lying enemies who expected to reap good for their shameful behavior toward him (vv. 1–5). As we have noted, Psalm 69:9 leaves the impression that David's passion for the temple created strong opposition among his compatriots and led to much emotional pain for him. Yet his commitment emboldens him to endure the scorn and bear the shame, especially since he recognizes that he bears it all "for your [Yahweh's] sake" (v. 7). That, of course, shifts the ultimate responsibility for David's actions to Yahweh, for he is persuaded that his cause is one and the same with Yahweh's; that is its redeeming power, enabling David to tolerate his opponents.

At the same time David's shame is graced by another redeeming force, his love for his people: "you who seek God, let your hearts revive. For the LORD hears the needy and does not despise his own people who are prisoners" (69:32–33). So powerfully commanding is this love that David asks the Lord to keep him from doing anything that would bring shame to the people of God: "Let not those who hope in you be put to shame through me, O Lord GOD of hosts; let not those who seek you be brought to dishonor through me, O God of Israel" (v. 6). The persona of David that we see in these psalms is that of one who has come to see Yahweh's cause to be his own ("the reproaches of those who reproach you have fallen on me," v. 9), and David's efforts to advance it, especially the building of the temple, is its highest expression.

As mentioned above, Psalms 69–71 form a cadre of psalms that facilitate the transition from Book 2 to Book 3. In 70:3 the psalmist accomplishes this in

---

6. Although Ps. 71 is not attributed to David, it continues the theme of shame that is so central in Pss. 69 and 70 and most likely should be considered Davidic. This pattern is represented also by Pss. 9–10, where Ps. 9 is attributed to David and Ps. 10 has no title, and Pss. 101–3, where Pss. 101 and 103 are attributed to David and Ps. 102 has no title but the content certainly sounds Davidic.

part by a slight rewording of 40:15, replacing the verb "be desolated" (*yashommu*) with "turn back in retreat" (*yashubu*). That change from "desolated" to "retreat" may suggest that in the new era represented by Book 2, David's fortunes have turned from being the victim to being the victor. It was shame that worked its power on David's situation, even though he still confessed his true identity, one which his beloved Israel needed to hear: "I am poor and needy" (70:6). Table 2 highlights the differences between these two texts.

Table 2. The Transition from Psalm 40 to Psalm 70

Psalm 40:13-16 (40:14-17 MT)	Psalm 70:1-4 (70:2-5 MT)
Be pleased, O LORD [Yahweh],	O God ['*elohim*],
to deliver me;	deliver me;
O LORD, help me quickly.	O LORD, help me quickly.
Let those be ashamed	Let those be ashamed
and confused together	and confused
who seek to end my life.	who seek my life.
Let those who desire to hurt me	Let those who desire to hurt me
withdraw	withdraw
and be disgraced.	and be disgraced.
Let them turn back [*shmm*, "be	Let them turn back [*shub*, "turn
devastated"]	back in retreat"]
because of their shame,	because of their shame,
those who say of me, "Aha! Aha!"	those who say, "Aha! Aha!"
Now the subject shifts from David's enemies to the faithful, as David prays that the faithful may have a life of joy.	
Let all those who desire you[, Lord,]	Let all those who desire you[, Lord,]
rejoice and be glad in you;	rejoice and be glad in you;
let all those who love your salvation	let those who love your salvation
say continually:	say continually:
"The LORD [Yahweh] is great!"	"God ['*elohim*] is great!"

Note: The translations are my own.

Other Angles of Shame in Psalms 69-71

We have already pointed out that the three webbing themes were picked up from Psalm 40. The NIV translates 40:15 as "be appalled at their own shame," evidently directing attention to the mockers' humiliation, while the verb "turn back" in 70:3 seems to hold out some hope that they will "turn away" from their insensitive behavior. Further, the omission of "to me" (40:15) in 70:3 (which the NIV restores[7]) moves the condemnation from the single person of David, as it was in 40:15, to the community in 70:3. In both instances, however, shame is a persistent dishonor. David's love for his people Israel is an underlying theme throughout the Psalter, and to bring shame on the people he loved was to bring shame on himself.

Shame and God's Reputation

In our world where so many servants of God, often in prominent positions, have experienced spiritual shipwreck and brought shame on themselves and on Christ and his church, David's prayer is one that we all should pray daily. Our first prayer, naturally, is that we not bring shame to ourselves personally. But the matter does not stop there, in the biblical world and ours as well, for shame is infectious and brings emotional suffering and social despair to those close to us. Paul admonishes the Ephesians "to walk in a manner worthy of the calling to which you have been called" (Eph. 4:1). God's reputation is paramount, and how we live out our faith and execute our ministries of grace reflects not only our own character but also, and more importantly, God's character. I often tell the story of my high school English teacher whose father was a Methodist pastor. One day she told us how, when she was a teenager and would go out at night with her friends, her mother would say, "Frances, remember whose daughter you are." I did not sense that the reminder raised any resentment in her—she recognized that her reputation and her father's were interlocked. That was a given, and she conducted herself in a manner that reflected her father's commitment to Christ and his church. This meant that she, her family, her church, and Christ were all honored in her behavior.

To bring shame on Christ and his church and the gospel we proclaim is a transgression of major proportions. Our reputation is tied to Christ and his gospel, and the way we conduct our lives reflects Christ's character. We are living letters, as Paul reminded the Corinthians: "And you show that you are a letter from Christ delivered by us, written not with ink but with the Spirit of the living God, not on tablets of stone but on tablets of human hearts" (2 Cor. 3:3).

---

7. This is one of those instances in the Psalms where the singular and plural are interactive, and Ps. 70 takes advantage of that, making the person of David the individual and the people he serves ("poor and needy") interchangeable.

The Demise of Shame

The demise of shame in Western culture is a signal that we have lost our moral underpinnings. One can argue that morality is a construct of the social and psychological forces of culture—it is not religious, or ought not to be. This argument stems from that time in Western history when the values of the Judeo-Christian worldview and its vertical/horizontal perspective were reduced to a horizontal range—there was no God with whom we must interact. Or if such a God did exist, this deity had an agnostic approach to human behavior. Along with that colossal loss came a gigantic adjustment in which humanity projected their own image as their deity. It was idolatry in its original version. Morality also was neutralized because cultural restraints became the "guardian angels" of this horizontal worldview, and shame became an unwelcome stranger.

The Gospel and Shame

Shame still remains a factor in our social and moral worlds, but it should be more a temporary than a permanent matter. Even though I have contended that shame can play a restitutive role in our social order and in the church, there is a most important truth that the Christian gospel presents to us: that Christ's sacrifice on the cross was the vicarious bearing of our shame so that Christ's forgiveness of our sins takes away the guilt and the shame. In Isaiah's words, the truth of the Old Testament gospel is that the Suffering Servant would vicariously bear our sins (Isa. 53:4–6), and Christ's redeeming death on the cross put this majestic plan into effect. Note the pronoun "our" in Isaiah's fourth Song of the Suffering Servant:

> Surely he has borne our griefs
>   and carried our sorrow;
> yet we esteemed him stricken,
>   smitten by God, and afflicted.
> But he was pierced for our transgressions;
>   he was crushed for our iniquities;
> upon him was the chastisement that brought us peace,
>   and with his wounds we are healed.
> All we like sheep have gone astray;
>   we have turned—every one—to his own way;
> and the LORD has laid on him
>   the iniquity of us all. (Isa. 53:4–6)

Among the theological profundities of the book of Hebrews, the cross and the intercession of Christ at the Father's right hand are the climax of redeeming grace. The two doctrines that enclose the reality of the cross are the joy that drew Christ to the cross and the shame he suffered because of it: "Therefore, since we are surrounded by so great a cloud of witnesses, let us also lay aside every weight, and sin which clings so closely, and let us run with endurance the race that is set before us, looking to Jesus, the founder and perfecter of our faith, who for the joy that was set before him endured the cross, despising the shame, and is seated at the right hand of the throne of God. Consider him who endured from sinners such hostility against himself, so that you may not grow weary or fainthearted" (Heb. 12:1–3).

Although our writer does not explicitly say that Christ endured the shame of the cross for us, it is quite clear from the book's theology that Christ had no sin, so the shame he bore was certainly not his: "For we do not have a high priest who is unable to sympathize with our weaknesses, but one who in every respect has been tempted as we are, yet without sin" (Heb. 4:15). Since shame has to have an object, and the shame represented by the cross and the sins Christ bore on it were not his, the logical conclusion is that the shame he bore was *ours*.

The extension of this doctrine to our personal and corporate life seems to follow logically: once we are forgiven through the gracious blood of Christ, shame for our forgiven sins does not follow as a consequence. That does not mean, of course, that forgiveness obliterates all remembrance of sin, but it wipes our conscience clean and puts us right with God. Our sins with their shame were all laid on Christ. The glorious truth is that we do not have to bear our shame because Christ bore it for us, the shame of the cross and the shame of our sins that put him there: "For our sake he made him to be sin who knew no sin, so that in him we might become the righteousness of God" (2 Cor. 5:21). When our sins trigger the painful power of shame—which is not unusual—we need to remind ourselves that Christ has already borne it for us. The initial tinges of shame can lead us to repentance, and repentance claims Christ's vicarious burden of shame. We don't have to endure it, nor do we have to endure the accusations of those who would foist it upon us. The gospel decrees that shame has no scarlet letter.

In the economy of the Christian gospel, shame is an instrument that leads to repentance and brings us to the reality that forgiven sin has no shame—regret, yes; remorse, certainly, but regret and remorse are different masters.

The taskmaster of shame has been relieved of his task, deprived of his authority: "Therefore, since we have been justified by faith, we have peace with God through our Lord Jesus Christ. Through him we have also obtained access by faith into this grace in which we stand, and we rejoice in hope of the glory of God. Not only that, but we rejoice in our sufferings, knowing that suffering produces endurance, and endurance produces character, and character produces hope, and hope does not put us to shame, because God's love has been poured into our hearts through the Holy Spirit who has been given to us" (Rom. 5:1–5).

ELEVEN

Weeping for the Night, but Joy in the Morning

Weeping and Joy (Pss. 30-33)

The Bible tends to speak in terms of opposites: night and day, good and evil, poor and rich, wicked and righteous, sorrow and joy, and the list could go on. Obviously our thought patterns are similar, but a case could be made that ancient people were more inclined than we are to utilize this pattern. Sociologically speaking, that is the way their world was divided. It was a class-laden society, and some of the sociological categories determined a lifetime of socioeconomic victimization for their citizens. Economically, the wide span between the rich and the poor was a reflection of that sociological division. There was no middle class in ancient Israel, except in very prosperous times—for example, the period of the prophet Amos (e.g., Amos 6:1–7)—and even then, such a "middle class" was a temporary phenomenon, more often than not achieved by fraudulent means, and did not have the security the modern American middle class has enjoyed.

Psalm 30 engages "weeping" and "joy" as its opposite categories, and in each of these words is a story of the psalmist's life experiences. While it is not always possible to put one's finger on the main idea of a psalm, Psalm 30 makes it easy for us. The major theme is clear in verse 5b: "Weeping may tarry for the night, but joy comes with the morning."

This psalm is an excellent example of the literary style that the psalmists sometimes deploy to develop their major themes. Here in Psalm 30 David does it in three ways. First, he rephrases the theme in equivalent sayings: "For his anger is but for a moment, and his favor is for a lifetime" (v. 5a); "You have turned for me my mourning into dancing" (v. 11a); "you have loosed my sackcloth and clothed me with gladness" (v. 11b). These statements say the same thing in different words. Second, the psalmist gives hints of the circumstances that caused his weeping and those that brought him joy. These elusive terms and phrases tell a general story. That is, David's weeping is related to the depths (of despair) caused by his enemies (v. 1), a brush with death (v. 3), and a sense of God's abandonment (v. 7), none of which he amplifies. The story of joy, in addition to the main theme, is enhanced by the psalmist in similar abbreviated terms: "mourning to dancing" (v. 11a); from wearing sackcloth to being clothed with joy (v. 11b); "that my heart may sing your praises and not be silent" (v. 12a). Third, the choice of vocabulary, especially the vocabulary of joy, is a literary feature that lightens the weight of lament and transforms David's numerous adverse circumstances into a life of joy. Psalm 30, for example, uses two verbs ("sing," *zmr*, and "rejoice," *smh*) and one noun ("joy," *rinnah*) to convey the idea of joy or rejoicing, and it is not coincidental that Psalms 31–33 are also charged with the vocabulary of joy, producing a cadre of "joyful psalms." The data in table 3 reveal the pattern of five verbs of joy and their derivative nouns as they weave their way through these four psalms.

Table 3. The Vocabulary of Joy in Psalms 31-33

Psalm 30	"sing" (verb, *zmr*, vv. 4, 12)
	"joy/rejoicing" (noun, *rinnah*, v. 5)
	"rejoice" (verb, *smh*, v. 11)
Psalm 31	"be glad" (verb, *gyl*, v. 7)
	"rejoice" (verb, *smh*, v. 7)
Psalm 32	(joyful) "songs" (noun from verb *rnn*, v. 7)
	"rejoice" (verb, *smh*, v. 11)
	"be glad" (verb, *gyl*, v. 11)
	"sing" [joyfully] (verb, *rnn*, v. 11)
Psalm 33	"sing joyfully" (verb, *rnn*, v. 1)
	"make music" (verb, *zmr*, v. 2)
	"sing" (verb, *shyr*, v. 3)
	"rejoice" (verb, *smh*, v. 21)

Given the feature of word associations that connects so many of the psalms under a common theme, we may assume that this thread of joy that connects Psalms 30–33 is intentional, and I would suggest that Psalm 30:5 is the beginning of that thematic thread. David wants us to know that inscribed on the lintel of his life is this motto: "Weeping may tarry for the night, but joy comes with the morning." He develops this theme in a masterful way.

Joyfully we should make this point. While our tears are usually undesirable, they carry a highly constructive purpose in our lives: they can be a moving force that transports us from sorrow to joy. That thought is present in the reflective lines of Psalms 30–33. It was in the depths of despair that the tears would have flowed when David's enemies had the upper hand (30:1), when death seemed near (30:2–3), and in the moments when the psalmist felt God had abandoned him (30:7). There is a Jewish saying that "there is no door through which tears do not pass."[1] In another psalm David prays, "You have kept count of my tossings; put my tears in your bottle" (56:8). Just as parents are moved by their child's tears, so God is moved by ours. Or perhaps we should turn the sentence around and say, as God is moved by his children's tears, so parents are also moved by their children's tears. The Levitical poet of Psalm 80 addresses God as the "shepherd of Israel" and in the same psalm credits God with feeding his people with the bread of tears (80:5), as the psalmist asks God three times to "restore us, O God; let your face shine, that we may be saved!" (80:3; cf. vv. 7, 19), pleading as one of the sheep of the Shepherd of Israel (80:1). It doesn't sound like the Shepherd meant his sheep any harm, but it was part of the saving plan to deliver them. Moreover, when the Judeans were returning from the Babylonian captivity, their songs of joy resounded along the journey home, giving the sense that their return was the harvest they had reaped for the seed they had sown in exile:

> When the LORD restored the fortunes of Zion,
>   we were like those who dream.
> Then our mouth was filled with laughter,
>   and our tongue with shouts of joy;
> then they said among the nations:
>   "The LORD has done great things for them."
> The LORD has done great things for us;
>   we are glad.

1. Westcott, *The Epistle to the Hebrews*, 128.

> Restore our fortunes, O LORD,
> like streams in the Negeb!
> Those who sow in tears
> shall reap with songs of joy!
> He who goes out weeping,
> bearing the seed for sowing,
> shall come home with shouts of joy,
> bringing his sheaves with him. (Ps. 126:1–6)

Their tears of sorrow had turned to tears of joy. Weeping had tarried for the night, and now the hues of morning's light were revealing God's radiant face.

A Verb Compacted with Joy

Words have histories, and our understanding of the Psalms is enriched when we inquire of those histories, while also recognizing that we must be careful not to overcharge any one stage of that history. For example, a sampling of Hebrew words for "praise" appears to derive from nouns that nuance physical parts of the human body or body movements, suggesting that certain acts of worship were accompanied by particular body gestures.[2] "To give thanks" or "confess" (*ydh*) appears to derive from the noun "hand" (*yad*), suggesting an extending of the hand that would have accompanied the spoken verb of thanksgiving; the verb "to bless" relates to the noun "knee" (*berek*), suggesting a bending of the knee may have accompanied a spoken blessing. There is another interesting word in the Hebrew vocabulary that is not a noun but is related to a body movement, the verb "to worship" (*hishtahaweh*), meaning "to bow down," suggesting the prostration of the worshiper as a sign of humility before the Lord: "Worship the LORD (*hishtahawu*) in the beauty of holiness" (Ps. 29:2 KJV). At some point the basic meaning of the verbs was disassociated from body parts and movements, and the terms functioned simply as worship vocabulary, although some were preserved in Christian traditions. In other instances some verbs acquired nuances that continued to be intentional.

---

2. This phenomenon seems to be more widely practiced than just in worship; e.g., the expression "to lift one's hand" is used as an idiom for "to swear." That is, swearing an oath was accompanied by lifting one's hand (e.g., Ps. 106:26).

There are also numerous words in the English language that we call onomatopoeia. They are words that mimic the sound their actions make. The
word "tick-tock" duplicates the sound of a clock, and "clap" approximates the
sound of hands slapping together. There are onomatopoetic words in Hebrew
too, but there is another division of words that does not match onomatopoeia
but carries a distinctive sound that has become so intimately associated with
the word that the word and sound are inseparable. The verb "make a joyful
noise/shout aloud" (*hari'u*, from root *rw'*) retained the nuance of joy that was
associated with the verb: "*Make a joyful noise* to the LORD, all the earth" (Ps.
100:1). Amos Hakham says this "shout" consisted of a high, staccato sound of
an instrument or human voice.[3] English translations, almost without exception, all the way back to Coverdale (AD 1535, "O be joyful in the Lord, all ye
lands"), have retained the nuance of joy that is inherent in this verb.[4] It was
a festal shout that was intended to celebrate a special festival or event (also
66:1; 95:1–2; 98:4), and the shout or sound was perceived as a joyful tone.
The joy and the high staccato sound have been associated with festal events
for so long that the celebrants find themselves dancing and singing with joy.
For the lack of an appropriate term, I have described this phenomenon as a
verb compacted with joy.

Joy, a Festal Garment

The theme of joy in the Psalter is presented in a beautiful metaphor as a garment that one wears, a garment indeed with which God clothes the worshipers. We might even describe God with the word "haberdasher," somewhat
out of vogue now but nevertheless quite appropriate for our purposes. The
joy-laden Psalm 30 attributes to the Lord the task of clothing David, reclothing
him in fact, with joy—that is, exchanging his mourning garments for joy: "you
[Yahweh] have loosed my sackcloth and clothed me with gladness" (v. 11).
Sackcloth was worn as a sign of mourning and deep sorrow, and David had
known sorrow's deepest abyss, more than any one person ought ever have to
know. For a man who had lost his infant son and whose grown son Absalom

3. Hakham, *The Bible: Psalms*, 1:368.
4. The King James Version of 1611 is typical: "Make a joyful noise unto the LORD." The
Geneva Bible of 1599 is the only exception I have found: "Sing ye loud unto the Lord, all the
earth"; but to the credit of the translators/editors, the footnote recognizes the verb's innate
nuance of "rejoice."

turned a revolutionary against his own father—for whom David would have given his own life—and a man who was driven out of his own capital city by a mutinous mob, for this man to have his mourning garments exchanged for the garment of joy would understandably prompt his vow to "sing your [Yahweh's] praise and not be silent" (v. 12). And our haberdasher God specializes in the finest line of spiritual clothing, supplying the accoutrements of life that can completely transform not only our outward appearance but our inward person, transforming us with saving faith. The Lord, says David, replaced his mourning clothes with joy. Note that—this is very important—God is overwhelmingly the subject of the verbs of Psalm 30. Our divine Clothier has other lines of fine wear in which he expertly fits his spiritual clients, but joy is at the top of the line.

Other imagery relates to this metaphor of the Lord clothing his people with joy. Whether or not there is a hint of the Lord's making coats of skins to clothe Adam and Eve, replacing their own makeshift garments (Gen. 3:21), the haberdasher metaphor nevertheless alerts the astute reader to that divine act of grace. Psalm 132 yearns for the priests to be clothed with righteousness and salvation (vv. 9, 16; cf. 2 Chron. 6:41), and David, reflecting on his military exploits, is aware that God clothed him with strength for the battle (Ps. 18:32, 39 = 2 Sam. 22:40).

Among the harvest festivals celebrated in Israel,[5] Tabernacles/Booths (Sukkoth) was instituted with a command that this festival be celebrated joyfully: "*You shall rejoice* [*smh*] before the LORD your God seven days" (Lev. 23:40); "You shall keep the Feast of Booths seven days, when you have gathered in the produce from your threshing floor and your winepress. *You shall rejoice in your feast*" (Deut. 16:13–14). The fact that the grape harvest was ripe at that time of the year and facilitated the celebration may have had something to do with the joy of the festival, but it was a joy deeper than wine and found only in a relationship with God. Artur Weiser comments on the increase of the harvest celebrated in Psalm 67:6: "The temporal things become the promise of the things that are eternal."[6] Amos describes this phenomenon that would mark the eschatological age by predicting that the harvests would be so abundant that one harvest would not have been fully gathered before the plowman appeared to ready the soil for the next planting: "'Behold, the days

5. The three harvest festivals are Passover/Unleavened Bread—barley harvest; Feast of Weeks—wheat harvest; and Tabernacles (Sukkoth)—grape harvest.

6. Weiser, *Psalms*, 477.

are coming,' declares the LORD, 'when the plowman shall overtake the reaper and the treader of grapes him who sows the seed'" (Amos 9:13).

The Joy of the Journey

One of the many metaphors the Psalms use to describe the believer's life and faith is that of a journey. Naturally, the psalmists use both verbs and nouns to say what they mean. For example, they use verbs such as "go in," "go out," "cross over," "go around," "go up," and "go down" to describe movements from one place to another. Nouns such as "feet," "path," "way," and "steps" join the glossary of mobility. From this plethora of words, the psalmists articulate their journey of life and faith. For them there are not two journeys but one, for life is faith and faith is life, a reflection of their theology that refuses to endorse the notion of a plurality of deities.[7] There are not numerous gods who help them on their way, but óne God, Yahweh. It is said that atheism was not known in the ancient Near East, even though Psalms 14 and 53 seem to endorse a version of philosophical atheism. Yet, the widespread nature of pantheism and polytheism in the ancient Near East leaves little room for the existence of philosophical atheism. Thus, the idea that these fraternal twin psalms are expressive of practical atheism, a world where people lived as if there were no god, makes sense.[8]

It is not coincidental that Psalm 1 distinguishes between two ways: "the way of the righteous" and "the way of the wicked" (v. 6). We could make a strong case that this is a general way to express the theology of the Psalter, and the rest of the book, speaking very broadly, may be viewed as the explication of these two ways. The master poet of Psalm 119, for example, sets out to distinguish the way of torah as the way of life and other non-torah ways as divergent paths that lead to death. While not distinguishing the two ways in clear categories as does Psalm 1, Psalm 119 lays them out in multiple metaphors and descriptors so that it is clear that his theological system resembles that of Psalm 1. In fact, the writer of Psalm 119, by the constant repetition of references to the Torah, draws out the same theme that we hear in Psalm 1, the meditation on the Torah over against the rejection of the Torah as the way of life.

7. See Bullock, "Yahweh and Other Gods in the Psalter," in *Psalms*, 1:54.
8. Bullock, *Psalms*, 1:98.

The Path's Landscape

The writers of the Psalms are fundamentally realists, especially as they scrutinize the path along which life's journey must be conducted. It is not always straight, although it should be; it is not always clear of obstacles, even though that makes travel easier and safer. But it is, first, lighted by God's word (*torah*), "a lamp to my feet and a light to my path" (119:105; cf. v. 11). This is one of the most helpful features of the pathway because pilgrims can see where they are going. Second, other accoutrements, generally moral in nature, enhance the security and provide directional assistance for sojourners: "Righteousness will go before him and make his footsteps a way" (85:13). Isaiah announces a "voice" crying in the wilderness: "In the wilderness prepare the way of the LORD; make straight in the desert a highway for our God" (Isa. 40:3). No ancient king would be allowed to travel without proper preparations, and that was the image Isaiah had in mind. The Levitical composer of Psalm 85 evidently had this same picture in mind when he drew the word picture of "righteousness" going before the Lord and making "his footsteps a way" (85:13). God walks the path he has prepared for his people.[9] This is a beautiful foreshadowing of the incarnation in this powerful psalm. Any path prepared by righteousness personified would reflect the character of the Monarch who would traverse this highway.

This is the journey of life and faith laid out by the psalmists, and the travel guidelines—more than guidelines, the rules of the road—are intended to turn the traveler into the likeness of the King to whom the highway belongs and who waits at the end of the journey to welcome the travelers home. The travelers themselves also establish a chronicle of the journey—the Psalms are our beloved copy—and leave it to inspire others who walk that path. Eugene Peterson says, "Christians tramp well-worn paths: obedience has a history."[10] In another context David confesses the joy of arrival: "As for me, I shall behold your face in righteousness; when I awake, I shall be satisfied with your likeness" (Ps. 17:15).

Hardly a better portrait of the King can be found in the Psalter than the sketch we have in Psalm 47. He is the great king over all the earth (vv. 2, 7) who reigns, not just over Israel, but over the nations (v. 8). The nations' princes have claimed Abraham's God as their own (v. 9)—he is the universal God. Yet,

9. Bullock, *Psalms*, 2:101.
10. Peterson, *A Long Obedience in the Same Direction*, 166.

God's sovereignty, celebrated in Psalm 47, provides the joyful climax of the journey. The list of God's attributes is notable: "the LORD, the Most High" (v. 2); a "great king over all the earth" (v. 2), who ascended his throne "with a shout" (v. 5); "our King" (v. 6), who "sits on his holy throne" (v. 8) and is "highly exalted" (v. 9).

We should think of Psalms 46 and 47 as companion psalms, with the apostrophe[11] at the end of Psalm 46 addressing the nations of Psalm 47. The context of creation in 46:1–3 provides the context for Yahweh's ascent to his appointed place of worship in Psalm 47. He ascends from creation (earth, mountains, and sea in 46:2–3)[12] to "his holy throne" (47:8). Reading the two psalms as companions reveals Yahweh's journey, the journey we also take, from creation to redemption, and the powerful presence of Yahweh is always our traveling Host ("The LORD of hosts is with us," 46:7). And thankfully, the end of the journey includes the nations who are now numbered among "the people of the God of Abraham" (47:9).

This is the path we follow, a landscape furnished with the incomparable presence of God the Creator, whose wonderful saving deeds are posted prominently and permanently along the highway. They include the election of Abraham, deliverance from Egypt, Yahweh's intractable covenant with Israel, guidance through the wilderness, and entry to Canaan. On the Christian side of this climactic history are the birth of Jesus, the cross, and the resurrection; we can join the celebration of all peoples who shout to God "with loud songs of joy" (Ps. 47:1). This stunning picture is a foreshadowing of John's magnificent portrayal of the new heaven and the new earth, or the new Jerusalem, as John calls the new creation in Revelation 21:9–27. This Jerusalem came down out of heaven from God and was the proper dwelling place for God, who redeemed the erring human race. In a symbolic sense, after John walked about Zion, counted its towers, and viewed its ramparts, much like the psalmist had instructed his generation to do (cf. Ps. 48:12–13), God's promise of the covenant formula is ultimately fulfilled. Leviticus 26:12

---

11. "Apostrophe" in the literary sense of an address to an inanimate object or someone too distant to hear the speaker.

12. In the troubled times of Israel's world—and ours—the "mountains" (land) that appeared when God separated the waters (Gen. 1:9–10), allowing the submerged mountains to appear, metaphorically threatened to slip back into the waters from which they emerged. That is, creation was moving in the reverse direction, but still, even though the world moves in the wrong direction, "we will not fear" because God is "our refuge and strength" (Ps. 46:1–3). This is a powerful assurance that characterizes our journey of faith.

promises, "I will walk among you and will be your God, and you shall be my people," and John reports, "And I heard a loud voice from the throne saying, 'Behold, the dwelling place of God is with man. He will dwell with them, and they will be his people, and God himself will be with them as their God. He will wipe away every tear from their eyes, and death shall be no more, neither shall there be mourning, nor crying, nor pain anymore, for the former things have passed away'" (Rev. 21:3–4).

David's optimistic assessment of life in Psalm 30:5 has been finally established as a theological reality in God's plan for humanity's redemption. Weeping, with all its immeasurable and incalculable sorrows, has yielded to the unfailing supremacy of divine love. Death, with its appalling attendants—mourning and crying and pain—has passed away with the old order of creation. And God's illuminating presence radiates the order of "all things new" (Rev. 21:5).

God's Installations along the Path (Ps. 107)

The Psalms call Israel to be observant of the installations along the highway as they—and we too—move along the journey of life and faith. These especially include the works that the Lord has performed throughout Israel's history, often expressed with the Hebrew word *niple'ot* ("wonders, wondrous works/deeds," stressing the astonishing and miraculous nature of the events). The literary artisan of Psalm 107 begins Book 5 with a call to give thanks for God's love (*hesed*): "Oh give thanks to the LORD, for he is good, for his steadfast love [*hesed*] endures forever!" (v. 1). The psalmist weaves this beautiful poem together with a refrain that occurs four times (vv. 8, 15, 21, 31): "Let them thank the LORD *for his steadfast love* [*hesed*], *for his wondrous works* [*niple'ot*] to the children of man!" To provide the finishing touch to the psalm, the psalmist combines God's love and wonderful deeds into a single plural noun for love, "loving deeds" (*hasidim,* plural of *hesed*): "Whoever is wise, let him attend to these things; let them consider the steadfast love of the LORD [*hasde Yahweh*]" (v. 43). That is, God's "wonderful deeds" performed on Israel's journey from Egypt to Jerusalem were done out of his "steadfast love," those terms occurring in parallel in the fourfold refrain. Israel could not, nor can we, avoid God's steadfast love, nor should we in our utmost fallenness even want to.

We should also note that the four circumstances Israel faced were times of desperation: (1) desert wastelands where they were hungry, thirsty, and dying, and desperately looking for a city to dwell in (107:4–5); (2) prisoners whose incarceration (exile) is a consequence of their rebellion against God (vv. 10–12); (3) people dying of hunger because of their rebellious ways (vv. 17–18); (4) seafarers whose lives are threatened by the perils of the sea (vv. 23–27). Israel's reaction to their circumstances was that "they cried to the LORD in their trouble," and the Lord's reaction to their desperate cry—and here's the essence of the wonder!—was that he "delivered them from their distress" (vv. 6, 13, 19, 28). These were the divine installations of God's love along Israel's highway of faith. They were seared in their memory. Or they should have been!

This psalm is really the message of God's steadfast love. Psalm 107 is in Book 5, the background of which is the return from exile and the reinstitution of worship in Jerusalem, including the rebuilding of the temple. The psalm, a marvelous thanksgiving psalm of love, was written with Israel's history in view, and the "poet laureate" of the return pens four scenarios of Israel's history (see the list above) that resonated with innumerable personal histories of God's people on their journey to a place to dwell. When Psalm 107 was written, these expatriates were probably home or packing their belongings for the long journey, secured by God's steadfast love (Ps. 106:47). Psalm 107 is the story of that love in miniature. It is the theological log of the journey. Psalm 126, then, is one for the historical archives, mingled with the laughter of almost fifty thousand returnees—commoners, priests, Levites, and servants ("our mouth was filled with laughter, and our tongue with shouts of joy," 126:2)—and filled with the joy of the Lord ("The LORD has done great things for us, and we are filled with joy," v. 3 NIV).

The geographical journey from Egypt to Jerusalem is both the historical pathway to joy, traveled under the leadership of Moses and Joshua, and the spiritual journey to the city of God as the people of Israel and individual believers of all ages travel in every generation. In the latter sense John the revelator's description of the new Jerusalem coming down out of heaven from God is the eschatological event of redeeming grace. The pattern of the Psalms is to describe from Egypt to Jerusalem for future generations, just as the writer to the Hebrews attributes Abraham's journey from Ur to Canaan as a much larger expedition, "for he was looking forward to the city that has foundations, whose designer and builder is God" (Heb. 11:10). It should not then surprise us that when David writes Psalm 23, his language usage reflects the major periods of Israel's trek from Egypt to Jerusalem.

The Destination That Shapes the Journey (Ps. 84)

Most of us would never start on a long journey without a clear destination in mind. In fact, the destination will be a determinative factor in many decisions along the way. We will need to know the route we should travel, what sites along the way are worth seeing, and what kind of weather we might encounter, to name only a few important considerations.

In terms of our spiritual journey, we have already spoken about the sites that are worth seeing along the way, which the psalmists often refer to as God's "great works" and God's "wondrous works/deeds." The backdrop of Psalm 84 is the journey to the temple, even though much of the psalm sounds like the pilgrims are already there. This "already but not yet" perspective is appropriate for the Psalms, as it is for people of every generation. Our attitude along the pathway is to be "as if" we had already arrived. We can never forget the true quality of faith, which is "the assurance of things hoped for, the conviction of things not seen" (Heb. 11:1).

The Levitical poet of Psalm 84 was one of the doorkeepers in the temple and reminisces about the privileges of his office: "I would rather be a doorkeeper in the house of my God than dwell in the tents of wickedness" (v. 10).[13] It may actually have been a menial task, but one day at this task was still "better than a thousand elsewhere" (v. 10). This psalm balances the privilege and joy of being officiants in the temple and the journey that brings them there. The joy of the temple, represented by the verb of verse 2 (*rnn*, "sing for joy"), is subsumed under the privilege of serving there, but joy and duty are compatible companions.

Our psalmist structures this lovely poem with three occurrences of "blessed" (*'ashre*), which, in this case, combine the joy and the privilege. Derek Kidner suggests that the first "blessed" (84:4), which concludes the first strophe (vv. 1–4), is made *longingly*: "Blessed are those who dwell in your house, ever singing your praise!" The psalmist, though a Levite, was not actually present in the temple but longed to be. The second "blessed" (v. 5) begins the second strophe (vv. 5–8) and, contends Kidner, is used *resolutely*: "Blessed are those whose strength is in you, in whose heart are the highways to Zion." The destination has so changed their character that the roads to Zion run right through their hearts. The journey has become an intimate part of them, and following Kidner's lead, we would say they are more resolute than ever—they

13. The Korahites were keepers of the temple gates (1 Chron. 9:17–27; Neh. 11:19).

have internalized the journey. The third "blessed" (v. 12) concludes the strophe of verses 9–12 and is used *contentedly*: "Blessed is the one who trusts in you."[14] The pilgrims' spiritual deportment and physical strength were shaped by the destination, to be in the temple, in the Lord's presence. We can summarize the three occurrences of "blessed" as the privileges of (1) being in the Lord's house; (2) journeying to the Lord's house; and (3) trusting in the Lord of the house.[15]

N. T. Wright comments that the Lord is committed to "re-create the world from within."[16] The pilgrims more and more reflect the Lord, who awaits them in the temple; their lives and journey have been shaped by the destination, because a longing for the house of the Lord is a longing for the Lord of the house. The psalmist has discovered, perhaps rediscovered, the joy of being in God's presence: "my heart and flesh sing for joy to the living God" (84:2), and that too has shaped the journey into one of joy. We see this reality in the life of our Lord in that the destination of the cross was the shaping power that made Christ's journey to Calvary an overwhelming joy—"who for the joy that was set before him endured the cross, despising the shame, and is seated at the right hand of the throne of God" (Heb. 12:2).

The Joy of Arrival

Sometimes the joy of the journey seems overwhelmingly more intense than the joy of arrival, but this may be more psychological than real. We have noted David's passion for the temple, which in the Psalms is equivalent to being in the presence of the Lord. This is captured beautifully in Psalm 23:6: "Surely goodness and mercy shall follow me all the days of my life, and I shall dwell in the house of the LORD forever." David was not a priest or Levite and would not have been able to spend his life in the temple, so he is evidently speaking about a spiritual state of being, although he certainly has in mind the temple he hoped to build. Further, David personifies "goodness" and "mercy" (*hesed*) as the double-powered engine that *pursues* him into the Lord's house.

---

14. Kidner, *Psalms 73–150*, 304.
15. Bullock, *Psalms*, 2:91, 93.
16. Wright, *The Case for the Psalms*, 91.

TWELVE

Waiting on the Lord

Two Verbs of Waiting

Two Hebrew verbs in the Psalms carry the idea of waiting.[1] The first has the nuance of waiting enduringly (*yhl*), which implies that the speaker faces hardships and is persevering as he waits longingly for the Lord to intervene: "But for you, O LORD, do I wait; it is you, O Lord my God, who will answer" (Ps. 38:15). In this psalm, David's moral failure underlies his troubles. The psalm is a depressive rehearsal of sin's social and spiritual effects.

The second verb (*qwh*) carries the sense of waiting expectantly, implying that the object of waiting is close at hand. David uses this verb to admonish Israel to wait for the Lord obediently ("and keep his way"), and they will be able to see the wicked cut off from the land of Canaan:

> Wait for the LORD and keep his way,
>> and he will exalt you to inherit the land;
>> you will look on when the wicked are cut off. (Ps. 37:34)

We have to appeal to context in order to determine the exact nuance of these verbs. Sometimes they occur in parallel lines, and in the case of Psalm 130:5, the second occurrence draws out the sense of hope by reference to God's word: "I wait [*qwh*] for the LORD, my soul waits [*qwh*], and in his word I hope [*yhl*]."

1. Wilson, *Psalms*, 636n5.

Strength and Courage: "Waiting for the Lord"

When we look at some of the beautiful literary constructions of important phrases and terms in the Psalter, we sometimes find a golden nugget that adds a special dynamic to a term. That is precisely the kind of structure we have in Psalm 27:14. Elsewhere I have compared the double occurrence of David's "wait for the LORD" to two strong arms that embrace the words of Moses to Joshua, "Be strong and courageous" (Josh. 1:6):[2] "*Wait for the LORD*; be strong, and let your heart take courage; *wait for the LORD*" (Ps. 27:14).

Part of the brilliance of the literary style is that the "embrace" of the call to "wait for the LORD" spells out the nature of the waiting: "Be strong, and let your heart take courage" (Ps. 27:14). It is a time to be strong and take courage, as Moses instructed Joshua to do when he faced the challenge of leading Israel in the conquest of Canaan. Waiting on the Lord is not a passive disposition. Rather, it requires an active engagement with the challenges and troubles that threaten the well-being of our relationship to the Lord. And so it is with David as he engages Moses's words and reaffirms that, for his situation as with Joshua's, the only hope of victory is to "wait for the LORD."

The prophetic voice of Isaiah similarly articulates the discipline of waiting: "they who wait [*qwh*] for the LORD shall renew their strength; they shall mount up with wings like eagles; they shall run and not be weary; they shall walk and not faint" (Isa. 40:31). The strength to run and not be weary, as any good runner knows, comes not by thinking about running but by practice and athletic engagement. Thus, as David prescribes in Psalm 27, we can be sure this strength of character did not develop in peaceful repose.

An Adverbial Modifier and Patient Waiting

While waiting often involves being active, it also requires patience. Patience means not hastening to a premature conclusion or action. At the same time, patient waiting does not mean tolerating anything that comes along. Patience comes when we recognize that there are things in life worth waiting for, persons we love who are worth tolerating until they can make needed changes to their attitudes and activities. Patience involves evaluating the gains and losses and electing to salvage a situation or person by waiting, a waiting which may involve tolerance, adaptation, and most of all, love.

2. Bullock, *Psalms*, 1:202.

We can draw on the power of language again when we hear David say, "I waited patiently [*qwh*] for the LORD; he inclined to me and heard my cry" (Ps. 40:1). In the Hebrew language there is an adverbial particle that precedes the main verb and imposes an urgency or intensification on that verb. A Hebrew verb doesn't like to be advised by a different Hebrew verb, so the adverb (called the infinitive absolute) must be from the same verbal root—it's a family affair. The psalmist could have said simply, "I waited [*qiwwiti*] for the LORD," but when he prefixes the adverbial modifier to the finite verb ("I waited"), the statement becomes more intense. Most English versions translate it: "I waited *patiently* for the LORD." The adverbial modifier intensifies the waiting, which is captured in our English translations as "patiently." But as discussed above, the entire psalm reveals that "patiently" is an active patience. And it has a power that regulates the psalmist's thoughts and activity when he finds himself in a slimy pit from which the Lord lifts him, when his personal sins trouble him and he prays for forgiveness, when his enemies hope to ruin his life—he waits patiently for the Lord with all of these concerns. The kind of "waiting on the LORD" the psalmist speaks about is one through which his faith grows stronger as he engages the destructive forces of life.

Waiting and Hope, Reflections of God's Steadfast Love

One of the beautiful observations about "waiting" and "hoping" in the Psalms is that they are essentially synonymous, sometimes engaging the same Hebrew verbs (*yhl* and *qwh*). The idea of "expectant waiting" or "waiting in faith" becomes equivalent to hope. M. A. C. Warren provides a metaphor that illustrates this well: hope is "faith on tiptoe."[3] That is, we stand on tiptoe, look across the troubles and obstacles that clutter our path, and see the glimmer, sometimes faint, of the things we are longing for. It is the kind of faith that Abraham had when he went to Canaan, "the land of promise," although it was a "foreign land" to him (Heb. 11:9). To use the metaphor of the writer to the Hebrews, this kind of waiting is "living in tents" though "heirs" of "the promise" (v. 9). It is not pretentious waiting, but one whose substance is not the "tents" we live *in* but the "promise" we live *with*. We could say that waiting on the Lord provides a telescope that brings our distant goal into clearer focus. By faith we live as if we already have realized the things we hope for.

3. Warren, quoted by Moule, *The Meaning of Hope*, 11.

We are among those "all who died in faith, not having received the things promised, *but having seen them and greeted them from afar*" (v. 13). Even then, the troubles and challenges of our momentary life are not obscured, but hope moves them to our peripheral vision and gives photographic clarity to our distant goal.

An excellent illustration occurs in Psalms 42–43, where the verb "to wait" (*yhl*) clearly means "to hope." The Levitical poet, with a kinship to the poet of Psalm 84, if not the author of both,[4] is stranded for an unknown reason in Galilee and unable to go to the temple. He recalls how he traveled with the pilgrims to Jerusalem to worship, recognizing that his longing was really for God: "As the deer pants for flowing streams, so pants my soul for you, O God" (42:1). Despite the verbal jibes of his compatriots (v. 3), the waiting becomes hoping, and hope becomes the theme of these companion psalms. The supplant engages in self-admonition: "Hope [*yhl*] in God; for I shall again praise him, my salvation and my God" (42:5–6, 11; 43:5). The psalmist's spiritual binoculars sharpen his gaze as he anticipates the reality of drinking from the flowing streams of God's presence in the temple.

The two verbs occur in sequence in Psalm 130, anchoring that hope in Yahweh's love:

> I wait [*qwh*] for the LORD, my soul waits [*qwh*],
>   and in his word I hope [*yhl*].
> . . . .
> O Israel, hope [*yhl*] in the LORD!
>   For with the LORD there is steadfast love [*hesed*],
>   and with him is plentiful redemption. (Ps. 130:5, 7)

Waiting enduringly and waiting expectantly cannot be isolated from the difficulties of our lives. Neither can waiting—specifically, waiting on the Lord—be isolated from hope. Waiting for the Lord moves us forward toward hoping in the Lord, and the telescopic lens of waiting directs our movement in that direction. The apostle Paul speaks of the creation that "waits with eager longing for the revealing of the sons of God. For the creation was subjected to futility, not willingly, but because of him who subjected it, in hope that the creation itself will be set free from its bondage to corruption and obtain the freedom of the glory of the children of God" (Rom. 8:19–21).

4. See Delitzsch, *Biblical Commentary on the Psalms*, 2:61.

While Psalm 96 does not speak of creation's "frustration," it nevertheless celebrates creation's joy in being liberated from its "bondage to decay":

> Let the heavens be glad, and let the earth rejoice;
>> let the sea soar, and all that fills it;
>> let the field exult, and everything in it!
> Then shall all the trees of the forest sing for joy
>> before the LORD, for he comes,
>> for he comes to judge the earth.
> He will judge the world in righteousness,
>> and the peoples in his faithfulness. (Ps. 96:11–13)

The psalmists' perspective brings the promised hope of God's world into clearer focus and summons the earth, in anticipation, to sing a new song (v. 1). Already the psalmist, standing on tiptoe, as it were, sees that eschatological day when the saints will sing a "new song," one whose message can be learned only by those who are beneficiaries of the sacrificial life of the Lamb of God (Rev. 14:3).

THIRTEEN

They Did Not Remember to Show Kindness

The Imprecatory Psalms Reconsidered

The imprecatory psalms have long been a source of contention among Psalms scholars and readers. The main question for Christians is how the psalmists and those of us who read the Psalms can unapologetically curse our enemies, particularly in light of our Lord's commandment that we should love our enemies and pray for them:

> You have heard that it was said, "You shall love your neighbor and hate your enemy." But I say to you, Love your enemies and pray for those who persecute you, so that you may be sons of your Father who is in heaven. For he makes his sun rise on the evil and on the good, and sends rain on the just and on the unjust. For if you love those who love you, what reward do you have? Do not even the tax collectors do the same? And if you greet only your brothers, what more are you doing than others? Do not even the Gentiles do the same? You therefore must be perfect, as your heavenly Father is perfect. (Matt. 5:43–48)

These psalms have been traditionally listed under the category of curses, which is the meaning of the word "imprecations." Some scholars have insisted that a change of classification would more correctly describe the psalms, and they have classified them as laments. They are laments, but the curses in them are certainly an obstacle to their full acclamation and acceptance. Even more drastic measures have been taken to reclassify them, with little resounding success.[1] I think some observations can help us look more favorably, even if begrudgingly, on these psalms. At least, we ought to explain their theological context and why they have a place in the Psalter.

The list of the psalms that are considered imprecatory, surprisingly, is rather long, including Psalms 35, 55, 59, 69, 79, 109, and 137. The three classic examples of imprecatory psalms are Psalms 35, 69, and 109, and as we might expect, they are all David psalms. These psalms share features, including (1) David's enemies did not care for the poor and needy (35:10; 69:33; 109:16, 22, 31), and (2) David was innocent, and his enemies had opposed him unjustly (35:7, 19; 69:4; 109:3). The enemies are vicious, and David describes them with choice metaphors: lions (35:17), snarling dogs (59:6, 14–15), bloodthirsty (59:2), and their words are drawn swords (55:21).

In ancient Near Eastern religion, the practice of cursing people and things was common. It was also part of Israel's faith, in some cases sanctioned by Yahweh, but we should note that the curses pronounced on Israel in Deuteronomy 27:9–26 involve violations of the Mosaic law. The bottom-line evil committed by David's enemies against him is that they "did not remember to show kindness, but pursued the poor and needy and the brokenhearted, to put them to death" (Ps. 109:16).

From David's Perspective

It is important to look at these psalms from David's perspective, which means combing through them to understand what he is saying about his enemies and about God. First, David is convinced of his innocence: they "attack me without cause" (Ps. 109:3; also 35:7, 19; 59:3; 69:4). This is the basic premise on which he launches his counterattacks. Second, the psalmist is confident of his kind behavior toward his enemies and laments that they repay him evil for good (35:12). Third, his perspective goes beyond his enemies, and he insists that he is suffering for God's sake: "For it is for your [God's] sake that I have borne reproach, that dishonor has covered my face" (69:7). Fourth, while his faith in his fellow human beings has been destroyed, his confidence in God is still in good condition, knowing that only God's steadfast love (*hesed*) can

1. See Bullock, *Encountering the Book of Psalms*, 222–26.

save him (109:21, 26). Indeed, the court of law is the picture we see in Psalm 109. The wicked man stands at the right hand of the accused; David is the defendant, while the wicked act as prosecutor (109:6). In the end, however, it is the Lord who stands at David's right hand as his defense attorney (109:31), and that signals David's victory over his enemies, a victory won by the Lord's intervention. Fifth, while his enemies were numerous, David affirms that he still had friends who believed in him; he values their loyalty and prays that he not violate their trust: "Let not those who hope in you be put to shame through me, O Lord GOD of hosts; let not those who seek you be brought to dishonor through me, O God of Israel" (69:6).[2]

The Nature of the Judgment

When we look at the judgment on his enemies for which David prays, generally it falls under the category of *lex talionis,* or the law of retaliation (Lev. 24:17–23). It reflects what I described earlier as the boomerang effect—that is, the offender's offense determines the gravity of the punishment (see "The Boomerang Effect of Evil" in chap. 8). David engages this principle in his prayer of Psalm 35:1: "Contend, O LORD, with those who contend with me; fight against those who fight against me!" And regarding the wicked one who is fond of cursing, so fond that he wears his cursing like a coat, David prays, "May it soak into his body like water" (109:18).[3] In the final analysis, however, the strategy of victory is found in the Lord's personal testimony on the defendant's behalf: "For he stands at the right hand of the needy one, to save him from those who condemn his soul to death" (109:31).

Are the Imprecatory Psalms Redeemable?

It is a bold question to ask of any Scripture whether it is redeemable, although there are, in practice, certain texts we do not use in Christian worship, simply because they do not comply with our social decorum. Yet, valiant attempts have been made to put the imprecatory psalms in a positive light, especially since they are a prominent part of Scripture. Without denying the challenge

---

2. These points are made in my chapter on the imprecatory psalms in *Encountering the Book of Psalms,* 226–28.

3. Biblical curses are not the language of profanity, as they are in modern English; they are wishes that bad things would happen to the object of hatred.

these psalms lay before us—a challenge I acknowledge and with which I have certain sympathies—efforts to defend these psalms highlight aspects that deserve our attention. C. S. Lewis reminds us that righteous indignation has a place in Christian society, and if the "curses" come under that heading, then they can sound the alarm of a decline of righteousness and moral conviction.[4]

Erich Zenger pays the imprecatory psalms tribute when he asserts that they give us a realistic view of the world, much like the Psalms generally, but these more intensely. Sometimes we need an outer force to wake us up. Further, he recognizes that the psalmists do not take vengeance into their own hands but leave it to God. The implicit message there may be that somewhere behind these psalms' assertions about humanity and evil, God's declaration "Vengeance is mine, I will repay, says the Lord" (Rom. 12:19) governs the thought of these poems. At least, there must be some restraining force that holds the psalmists back from retaliation. Says Zenger, "They leave *everything* in God's hands, even feelings of hatred and aggression."[5] If we can take our comments that far, then these psalms serve a purpose, even though we might wonder why they could not say it outright. But we may attribute this to the nature of poetry itself.

These observations hopefully can help us see the imprecatory psalms in a positive light and recognize that they can be instructive in teaching, reproof, correction, and righteousness, "that the man of God may be complete, equipped for every good work" (2 Tim. 3:17). At the same time, we must be careful not to overrate them as a clear directive concerning our own worship. Geerhardus Vos believed that they should have a place in Christian worship, especially since they are part of Scripture.[6] My word of caution is that if we use these psalms in Christian worship, we should use them alongside our Lord's teaching to love our enemies and pray for them (Matt. 5:43–48). The Old Testament ethic has a broad range that runs from "eye for eye, tooth for tooth" (Exod. 21:24) to the elevated plane of "love your neighbor as yourself" (Lev. 19:18). In the Sermon on the Mount our Lord describes a kingdom that operates according to a higher ethic, a kingdom where the two great commandments (Matt. 22:34–40) become the governing principles of redeemed society. When Jesus proclaims that all the Torah and the Prophets hang on those two commandments, the kingdom of God comes clearly in view.

4. Lewis, *Reflections on the Psalms*, 30.
5. Zenger, *God of Vengeance?*, 79.
6. Vos, "The Ethical Problem of the Imprecating Psalms."

PART 3

REDEMPTION

FOURTEEN

All in the Family: "For His Name's Sake"

The Life Setting of "For His Name's Sake"

"For his name's sake" is a phrase in the Psalter and shared by the Prophets that can be mystifying. Sometimes, unfortunately, we just move past it without recognizing its importance, or we sense it must be packed with theological value that will challenge our ability to comprehend, so we acknowledge it and move on. Although this phrase may indeed represent theological territory where angels fear to tread, I can offer a proposal that helps me, and hopefully my readers, appreciate the majesty and the mystery of this phrase.

When the psalmists use the phrase "for his [Yahweh's] name's sake," they are often speaking, to use the German phrase, about the *Sitz im Leben* (the "setting-in-life") of the phrase. I propose this setting is family life. More specifically, they are speaking from within Israel's covenant relationship to Yahweh. In either case, it is an in-house matter. It is the Covenant-Maker in the covenantal setting, or the family head in the social setting, who establishes the protocols and nurtures, by his own character and example, the nature of the family and how they are to present themselves to God, to each other, and to the world. It follows that Israel, both corporately and personally, is called upon to recognize and accept their responsibility to reflect and live out the character of the Covenant-Maker or the family head, whichever "setting-in-life" we are working with. In both cases, it is "all in the family."

First, we need to acknowledge that to honor God's name is to honor God. Names have significance in the Bible that surpasses the kind of role they play in our Western world. Bible names often represent one's true character, or what one was expected to become in life, or some family relationship, or some event that God is performing in the world. Hosea's children, for example, receive symbolic names that represent God's actions in Israel: a son named "Jezreel," because, says the Lord, "in just a little while I will punish the house of Jehu for the blood of Jezreel, and I will put an end to the kingdom of the house of Israel. And on that day I will break the bow of Israel in the Valley of Jezreel" (Hosea 1:4–5); a daughter named "No Mercy [Lo' Ruhamah]," because, says the Lord, "I will no more have mercy on the house of Israel, to forgive them at all" (v. 6); and a third child named "Not My People [Lo' 'ammi]," because, says the Lord, "you are not my people, and I am not your God" (v. 9). Then when the Lord reverses the plan represented by the ominous names, he instructs the prophet to change the children's names: "Say to your brothers, 'You are my people ['ammi],' and to your sisters, 'You have received mercy [ruhamah]'" (2:1).

To profane God's name was to rob him of his character, deprive him of his essential nature. That is, at least partially, the reason behind the commandment "You shall not take the name of the LORD your God in vain" (Exod. 20:7 = Deut. 5:11). The other side of this coin is in Deuteronomy 32, where the Lord says of Israel that he would "wipe them from human memory"—that is, annihilate them—were it not for the fact that he "feared provocation by the enemy, lest their adversaries should misunderstand, lest they should say, 'Our hand is triumphant, it was not the LORD who did all this'" (32:26–27). It is no less than the desecration of God's character that idolatry epitomizes, replacing God's character with an illicit proxy (see chap. 9, "We Become Like Our God"). It is the same concern the Lord had with his reputation when he spared the rebellious Israelites, newly delivered from Egypt: "But I acted *for the sake of my name*, that it should not be profaned in the sight of the nations among whom they lived, in whose sight I made myself known to them in bringing them out of the land of Egypt" (Ezek. 20:9).

The book of Deuteronomy has a prominent "Name" theology incorporated in the phrase "for the sake of his/your name," and its variants in the Psalter and Prophets[1] may represent an interdependence of Deuteronomy

---

1. The phrase also occurs as spoken *to* the Lord: "for your name's sake" (Pss. 25:11; 31:3; 79:9; 109:21; 143:11; Jer. 14:7, 21); "for the sake of your steadfast love" (Pss. 6:4; 44:26); as spoken *of* the Lord: "for his name's sake" or "for the sake of his righteousness" (Ps. 106:8; Isa.

and the prophetic witnesses. Further, the use of family terminology, such as "Father" for God and "children" for members of the covenant family, is common in the Psalter. In Psalm 89:26 David calls God his Father: "You are my Father, my God, and the Rock of my salvation" (see also 2 Sam. 7:14); and in Psalm 2 God himself acknowledges his fatherhood, using the verb "to beget": "You are my Son; today I have begotten [*yld*] you" (Ps. 2:7).[2]

The family metaphor is so beautifully applied to God's love in Psalm 103:13, and most appropriately, since David, to whom the psalm is attributed, was a father who loved his children, sometimes to the point of overindulging them: "As a father shows compassion to his children, so the LORD shows compassion to those who fear him." In Psalm 68:5 God is called "Father of the fatherless and protector of widows," revealing his compassion on those who have no father and on widows who are at the mercy of their extended families and often destitute without a husband to provide for them and their children.

While stressing the significance of names in biblical days as compared to today, we nonetheless still appreciate a correct and respectful use of our names. It makes us feel accepted and at home. When I enrolled for my first semester of seminary, I was working my way through the registration line, meeting various people involved in the registration process, and came to the dean of the seminary, who greeted me and said, "How are you, Mr. Bullock?" I had never seen this man in my life, but the dean of the seminary knew my name, had memorized it from the photo in my application folder. I was quite moved and felt like I already knew someone in the seminary, although I was in a totally new place with people I had never met. But someone knew my name.

The language of covenant and family overlaps. In fact, the Shema of Deuteronomy 6:4–9 is a teaching instrument intended for use within the family unit. Moses instructs Israel, corporately and individually:

> Now this is the commandment—the statutes and the rules—that the LORD your God commanded me to teach you, that you may do them in the land to which you are going over, to possess it, that you may fear the LORD your God, you and your son and your son's son, by keeping all his statutes and his commandments, which I command you, all the days of your life, and that your days may

---

42:21); as spoken *by* the Lord: "for the sake of my name" or "for my own sake" (Isa. 43:25; 48:11; Ezek. 20:9, 14, 22, 44); as spoken *by* the Lord and including David: "for my own sake and for my servant David's sake" (2 Kings 19:34; Isa. 37:35).

2. The Hebrew verb *yld* in Ps. 2:7 occurs in the *qal* stem and means "to beget," used of male persons; when used of female persons in the *hiphil* stem it means "to give birth."

be long. . . . You shall teach them diligently to your children, and shall talk of them when you sit in your house, and when you walk by the way, and when you lie down, and when you rise. (Deut. 6:1–2, 7)

Quite beautifully, Psalm 119 references the covenant relationship by assigning the role of teacher to Yahweh, who imparts the torah to his students. For example, in the same fashion that Yahweh was the real King of Israel and those earthly monarchs who sat on the throne were merely his representatives, for the suppliant of Psalm 119 Yahweh was the real Teacher and the human parents merely his representatives. Further, in keeping with the strong verbal nature of the Hebrew language, the poet of this psalm always depicts Yahweh's teaching role verbally—for example, verse 12: "teach me your decrees."[3] With such a Master Teacher, the educational value is magnified, both in its truth and in its authority.

Our point here is to show how instruction in the torah, the covenant teachings, was largely a family responsibility. We can extrapolate that when the psalmists use the phrase "for his [Yahweh's] name's sake," the setting-in-life is the family, and Yahweh is the family head who acts to protect and secure his own reputation; and the children (Israel), by deduction and by explicit instruction (Deut. 6:4–9), are responsible for transmitting that reputation to their offspring.

Our Western sense of individualism creates an obstacle for many of us, because we are encouraged to fulfill our own personal dreams and not necessarily those that our parents have for us. There is nothing wrong with this life philosophy per se, but sometimes it distances us from the solid instruction in Christ that faithful parents have given us. There is a point in our personal experience when we have to decide whether the fifth commandment to "honor your father and mother" (Exod. 20:12) binds us to their religious instruction. We are here working under the assumption that transmitting and protecting the reputation of Father Yahweh of our household, whose character is steadfast love with righteousness and justice, is our loving duty. William Wordsworth speaks of that kind of duty in his beautiful poem, "Ode to Duty":

3. "Teach me" is one of the major prayer petitions of the suppliant of Ps. 119. The psalmist always uses the *piel* imperative of the verb *lmd* (the *qal* stem means "to learn," and the *piel* stem expresses the causative sense, "cause me to learn" = "teach me" [*lammedeni*], occurring seven times in Ps. 119: vv. 12, 26, 64, 66, 68, 108, 135), except once the *hiphil* stem of the verb *yrh* ("direct," in the sense of "teach") occurs in v. 33.

> Stern Lawgiver! yet thou dost wear
> The Godhead's most benignant grace;
> Nor know we anything so fair
> As is the smile upon thy face.

Sadly, we often consider duty an incumbrance rather than a joyful privilege, and in view of this social disorder we can begin to make a change in our perspective.

Yahweh's Actions "For His Name's Sake"

The most frequent occurrence of our phrase in the Psalter is the simple "for his/your name's sake."[4] A verbal qualifier precedes the phrase, such as "leads/guides," "forgives," "saves," and "gives life."

Yahweh Guides

The image of Yahweh as Guide fits our setting-in-life very well, for it is the head of the family who, by the medium of instruction as well as example, provides guidance for the children. The NIV reflects the sense of the introductory clause of Psalm 31:3: "Since [*ki*, "because"] you are my rock and my fortress, *for the sake of your name* lead [*nhh*] and guide [*nhl*] me." These two verbs are also used in Psalm 23:2–3: "he *leads* [*nhl*] me beside quiet waters," and "he *guides* [*nhh*] me along the right paths *for his name's sake*" (NIV). The picture of Psalm 23, and likely also Psalm 31, is that of the Shepherd who, knowing the way, goes ahead of the sheep and leads them to quiet waters, and the sheep follow. God's leading his people "for his name's sake" (23:3) indicates that God acts in his own self-interests, or he acts in ways that protect his own reputation (see Ezek. 20:9, 14, 22), as any good shepherd would. Theologically speaking, God's actions in his own self-interest are expressions of his eternal nature. And because God is loving and compassionate, we can be sure that those actions, like forgiveness of our sins, are in our best interests as well. "For his name's sake" is not about a self-centered God, unless we understand "self-centered" to refer to a God who is loving and gracious and seeks to impute his reputation in the lives of his human creation—what a transfer! This latter understanding, to be sure, is the intended meaning of this phrase.

4. Pss. 23:3; 25:11; 31:4; 79:9; 106:8; 109:21; 143:11.

The metaphor of the shepherd leading the sheep in ways and to places that reflect the shepherd's own character takes a slightly different turn in Psalm 23:6 when "goodness and mercy" personified, major attributes of the Person of God, *drive* the sheep into the house of the Lord. The image of the shepherd in verse 6 is of one who comes behind the sheep driving rather than leading them home: "Surely goodness and mercy shall *follow me* [in pursuit; *rdp*]." Both metaphors are appropriate because sheep sometimes need to be driven into the fold rather than led.

Yahweh Forgives

At the heart of the Psalms is God's forgiveness of his human subjects, even though they willfully and unwillfully sin against him. In two instances the phrase "for your name's sake," spoken directly to God, attributes the psalmist's confidence in God's power and predilection for forgiveness to God's regard for his own name. At the same time, however, since God's human subjects are the grateful recipients of forgiving grace, concern for God's reputation and concern for ours are inseparable: "*For your name's sake*, O LORD, pardon my guilt, for it is great" (Ps. 25:11). David petitions God to live up to his reputation as the forgiving God. Significantly, David immediately precedes this petition with a description of Yahweh's character as described in the formula of grace, speaking of Yahweh's loving (*hesed*) and faithful (*'emet*) paths (Exod. 34:6). The medieval commentator Rashi remarks, "It is appropriate for the Great [God] to pardon Great Iniquity."[5]

Psalm 79:9 carries a treasured nuance in the phrase under consideration. The psalmist speaks to Yahweh in parallel lines about the "glory of your name" and "for your name's sake":

> Do not remember against us our former iniquities;
>> let your compassion come speedily to meet us,
>> for we are brought very low.
> Help us, O God of our salvation,
>> *for the glory of your name;*
> deliver us, and atone for our sins,
>> *for your name's sake!*
> Why should the nations say,
>> "Where is their God?" (Ps. 79:8–10)

5. Gruber, *Rashi's Commentary on the Psalms*, 270.

It is in the act of forgiveness that God clears Israel's past record of sins and then performs the act of deliverance upon that clean slate, just as if they had not sinned. The effect is that God manifests his self-interest—his reputation—so the nations won't interpret Israel's desperate need as divine impotence.

Yahweh Saves

Psalm 106 is a magnificent poem that celebrates Yahweh's grace as a response to human sin. The psalm is evidently a congregational psalm of thanksgiving, beginning with the plural imperative verb "hallelujah!" ("Praise the Lord"). The call to thanksgiving is also a plural verb form: "Give thanks" (*hodu*), and the psalm ends with a plural request: "Save us, O Lord our God, and gather us from among the nations, that we may give thanks to your holy name and glory in your praise" (v. 47). Four historical vignettes follow a thematic form: Israel sinned, and the Lord saved. Not surprisingly—but oh, how wonderful!—the response to Israel's sinning was Yahweh's saving. The first vignette (vv. 6–12), focused on Egypt and the Red Sea, includes the declaration that the Lord "saved them *for his name's sake*" to reveal his power (v. 8). While the other vignettes (the wilderness, vv. 13–23; sending spies into Canaan, vv. 24–33; and Israel's failure to destroy the Canaanites, vv. 34–45) do not include the phrase, the Lord's saving response is the same, and likely the psalmist views the phrase "for his name's sake" in verse 8 to be an all-encompassing theme for all four scenarios.

Trying to put the pieces of God's saving plan together in a composite whole is a wonderful challenge—wonderful in the sense that God has a saving master plan that underwrites the entire biblical story. John reflects that master plan in his loving affirmation:

> I am writing to you, little children,
> > because your sins are forgiven *for his name's sake.*
> I am writing to you, fathers,
> > because you know him who is from the beginning.
> I am writing to you, young men,
> > because you have overcome the evil one.
> I write to you, children,
> > because you know the Father.
> I write to you, young men,
> > because you are strong,

> and the word of God abides in you,
> and you have overcome the evil one. (1 John 2:12–14)

John reaches all the way back to the beginning and affirms the power of forgiveness *for Christ's sake*. He gives us a picture of the master plan that is invoked by the power of Christ's forgiving love.

Yahweh Preserves Life

Yahweh as the source of life is a truth that permeates the entire Bible. Needless to say, the seed bed of God as life's source and sustainer is Genesis 1–3. In the context of the incarnate Word, and in keeping with John's literary eloquence and theological clarity, John's Gospel traces the light of the gospel to the beginning and declares, "All things were made through him, and without him was not anything made that was made. *In him was life, and the life was the light of men*" (John 1:3–4). Thus the gospel flowed from the Word that was life and called light into existence. Christ affirms this in his pronouncement, "I am the light of the world. Whoever follows me will not walk in darkness, but will have the light of life" (John 8:12). The one instance in the Psalms that attributes the sustenance of life for Yahweh's own sake is Psalm 143:11–12: "For your name's sake, O LORD, preserve my life! In your righteousness bring my soul out of trouble! And in your steadfast love you will cut off my enemies, and you will destroy all the adversaries of my soul, for I am your servant." Yahweh's acts for his own name's sake are in the best interests of his own nature—that is, to communicate who he is—and by extension, in the best interests of his servants.[6] The outcomes of life and providence are synonymous, so we can confidently entrust our lives to Yahweh.

The Completion of the Family Circle

The mysterious and majestic phrase before us, "for your [Yahweh's] name sake," is a theological grid that the psalmists and prophets lay down for the progressive building of the great cathedral of Christ's love. The master plan was to bring believers into total compliance, indeed the mirror image of Jesus

---

6. See Bullock, "For His Name's Sake," in *Psalms*, 1:169.

Christ. The goal is not to make us into little gods—that would be idolatry—but to conform us into the image of Christ, who is the image of God.

In addition to using the language of conformation, Paul also speaks of a transubstantiation from our spiritual poverty to the richness of God's grace: "For you know the grace of our Lord Jesus Christ, that though he was rich, yet *for your sake* he became poor, so that you by his poverty might become rich" (2 Cor. 8:9). At first, the turn of the phrase from "for his [Yahweh's] sake" to "for your [the believers'] sake," a turn that also occurs in the Psalms, sounds like a 180-degree turn, but in the theology of the cross it was the self-projection of his own Person, God's love projected in his suffering. In Philippians 1:29 Paul turns the light back upon Christ revealed in the cross and acknowledges that we are called to suffer for Christ, just as he suffered for us: "For it has been granted to you that *for the sake of Christ* you should not only believe in him but also *suffer for his sake.*" While our suffering *for Christ's sake* is not redemptive as the Savior's is, it is reflective of his suffering and a witness to Christ's absolute redeeming grace and brings us into the ultimate reality of saving grace: "The Spirit himself bears witness with our spirit that we are children of God, and if children, then heirs—heirs of God and fellow heirs with Christ, provided we suffer with him in order that we may also be glorified with him" (Rom. 8:16–17).

When Paul considers what suffering for Christ's sake produces, he says what he has lost is like rubbish, and what he gains is "the surpassing worth of knowing Christ Jesus my Lord" (Phil. 3:8). The Lord Jesus put this truth in different but memorable words: "Whoever finds his life will lose it, and whoever loses his life *for my sake* will find it" (Matt. 10:39; cf. 16:25). This is the picture of "your will be done, on earth as it is in heaven" (6:10).

The Lord assured Israel through his prophet Isaiah that he was committed to this plan of reproducing his character, an image he had stamped on every human life. Amazingly, he made it very personal by the gift of the virgin's son, keying into the family design by promising a new family, a child born of a woman and named with the intimate name *'Immanu'el*, "God with us" (Isa. 7:14). God's design for humanity was to make the family the social centerpiece: Adam and Eve, Noah and his wife, Abraham and Sarah, and now a new mother and child. The plan was conceived in love, transacted in grace, and accomplished in faithfulness. Indeed, righteousness and love are not attributes that God imposes on us to make himself look good—he is good!—but they are an index to who he is, a thumb index to his character. And he, our haberdasher God,[7] seeks by his steadfast love to do for us what he did for the Edenic pair (Gen. 3:21): to clothe us by grace with his attributes of righteousness and love. Truly, we are God's namesake, named after God by his own design that he created in his "image," and we are to reflect his character, to respect and perpetuate his reputation, which is ours too because we are his children. It's all in the family, and the family is one with our God, and we by grace become like our God. It's all *for his name's sake.*

Abraham Kuyper looks back to the key reality of our creation in God's image and comments:

> Thus, *not for your sake but for God's sake,* religion is founded in your creation after the image of God. Your serious practice of the hidden walk with God is to realize the purpose that was expressed in your creation after His image.
>
> For though it is true that this exalted endowment renders you supremely rich, happy and blessed, though it anoints you priest and king, baptizes you as [a] child of God, and enriches you as a princely creature in the sanctuary; yet you fail dismally if you take this to be the root of the matter.
>
> First in rank and order here also is not what makes you blessed, but that which causes your God to accomplish His purpose; and that purpose always is that He wills to be known, loved, sought and worshiped; that He wills to have conscious, worshipful fellowship offered Him at the hand of His creation; that He wills not merely to be great, but to be known, as such, and believed, and loved.[8]

Psalm 143 lays out three theological strands that describe the phrase "for your name's sake": "in your faithfulness," "in your righteousness," and "in your steadfast love" (vv. 1, 11–12). If singly they are immeasurably strong, then just think how strong the woven cord would be. This is the cord that tethers David and all believers to the God of grace. And it is with this cord that Yahweh preserves our life "for his name's sake." It should not be lost on the reader that David alludes to Yahweh's often-cited attributes of faithfulness and steadfast love. In Psalm 143, they form an inclusio (vv. 1, 12). This feature puts the psalm and all believers, who are also Yahweh's servants, within the context of the second Sinai covenant. And we are called upon to reflect his character. It is all in the family.

---

7. See my explanation in "Joy, a Festal Garment" in chap. 11.
8. Kuyper, *To Be Near unto God,* 70.

FIFTEEN

Finding God in the Fabric of the World

In John Calvin's commentary on the Psalms, he reminds us that "it is in the fabric of the world that we meet God."[1] The axiom seems so evident it ought not surprise us, and when we think about meeting God, we can add the complementary axiom that "it is in the fabric of the world that God meets us," the incarnation being his supreme engagement. Frank Mason North in 1905 published his hymn "Where Cross the Crowded Ways of Life" and affirmed that it is in the crossroads of our world that we hear the voice of Jesus:

> Where cross the crowded ways of life,
> where sound the cries of race and clan,
> above the noise of selfish strife,
> we hear thy voice, O Son of Man!

John, of course, mapped out the path that God from eternity had planned, as Jesus Christ stepped onto the stage of history in human form: "And the Word became flesh and dwelt among us" (John 1:14).

But the fabric of the world is often troublesome and undisciplined, creating doubts and fears. For example, in Psalm 18:1–2 David cuts his terms for God's work in his life from the fabric of his world, from his military exploits, no

---

1. Calvin, *Commentary on the Book of Psalms*, 4:146.

less: my strength, my rock, my fortress, my deliverer, my shield, the horn of my salvation, and my stronghold. Yet, in David's world as in ours, war is an unending intruder, and God chooses to speak to us both through war, which is not his native tongue, and through peace, which is indeed his vernacular language. Through both he molds us into those vessels of service that bear the scars of our troubled lives. Yet, these mended wounds are turned by God's grace into scars of victory, like those scars of "a Lamb standing, as though it had been slain," the marks of the cross still present in his resurrected body (Rev. 5:6).

Psalm 104 is a marvelous picture of divine providence, which is really what we are talking about when we speak of meeting God in the fabric of the world. After the psalmist has introduced the profile of the majestic God, "clothed with splendor and majesty" as the Creator of the world (vv. 1–9), he opens up a lovely picture of a world crowded with the flora and fauna of God's creation (vv. 10–30), in which "man goes out to his work and to his labor until the evening" (v. 23). We human creatures are more central in the Psalms generally than we are in Psalm 104, where humanity is a minor figure in the massive world drama. J. J. Stewart Perowne makes an incisive statement on this psalm, commenting that in Genesis 1 we have a "still life" picture of the world, but in Psalm 104 we have a picture "crowded with figures full of stir and movement."[2] Perowne's lovely prose is worth repeating:

> The wild ass roaming the sands of the wilderness, stooping to slake his thirst at the stream which God has provided; the birds building their nests, and breaking forth into song in the trees which fringe the margin of the torrent-beds; the wild goats bounding from rock to rock, and finding their home in the inaccessible crags; the young lions filling the forest by night with their roar, and "seeking from God their prey"; and the sea with the same plentitude of life, its depths peopled with huge monsters and swarming myriads of lesser fish, and its surface studded with sails, the image of the enterprise, the traffic, the commerce of the world; and lastly, in fine contrast with this merely animal activity of creatures led by their appetites, the even tenor, the calm unobtrusive dignity of man's daily life of labour: take all these together, and we have a picture which for truth and depth of colouring, for animation, tenderness, beauty, has never been surpassed.[3]

2. Perowne, *The Book of Psalms*, 2:233.
3. Perowne, *The Book of Psalms*, 2:233.

It is into the fabric of that world with all its glory and mystery that our majestic Creator God enters.

But we earthlings cannot talk about the fabric of that world without thinking about the suffering that humanity must endure. Of all our theological challenges, this, it seems to me, is at the top of our list. It is this issue that elicits the anguished question of Psalm 22:1: "My God, my God, why have you forsaken me?" The psalmists face this question head-on, in all of its painful and ugly dimensions. Sometimes they simply let it stand on its own merits without trying to theologize its reality. At other times they cannot resist the opportunity to put a different face on suffering, recognizing that God is there in the midst of it with its human subjects—we are never alone. The question of suffering prompts an insightful comment from Artur Weiser: "Suffering, as it were, is capital invested with God, booked by him (cf. Mal. 3:16; Job 19:23) and collected by him."[4] We have no more profound version of this view than Joseph's response to his brothers' evil actions against him: "You meant evil against me, but God meant it for good, to bring it about that many people should be kept alive, as they are today" (Gen. 50:20). Whether or not God was the initiator of the brothers' evil deeds or just allowed them is an open question in the narrative. The story is told in such a way that it is impossible to unravel the evil deeds and their instrumentation for accomplishing God's good plan for his people. God is "the Master Weaver. Whether it was 'booked by him'—that is the difficult question—it was certainly 'collected by him.'"[5]

Suffering is the unwelcome and uninvited guest that visits us in the fabric of our world, and God has his way of showing us that he is the Master of the house. Whatever the intention of our uninvited guest, the Master of the house sees that the master plan is accomplished, whether that be in our present world or in the world to come.

Designed and Decreed by God (Gen. 1)

There are instructive clues in the early chapters of the biblical revelation that point the way toward God's majestic entrance into history in the person of Jesus of Nazareth—a truth that is cloaked in the creation narrative in the

4. Weiser, *Psalms*, 424.
5. Bullock, *Psalms*, 2:256.

phrase "the image of God." As we have emphasized earlier in our study,[6] God's self-commitment to his creation—in time and eternity—is inherent in that phrase. It is in the nature of that commitment that the Creator meets us, as he engages with humanity, his highest work of creation and the only one that reflects his personal nature.

The creation narrative of Genesis 1 builds to a climax. Immediately after the declaration that God created humankind in "the image of God," male and female (Gen. 1:27), the blessing of offspring—itself a creative act that God shares with humanity—and the divine mandate to "fill the earth" are connected with the mandate to "subdue" it (v. 28). The scope of human dominion extends over plant and animal life (v. 28), and then the narrative peaks when God pronounces everything he had made "very good" (v. 31). The human connection to the nonhuman creation is an inescapable fact. Most probably, we should take these mandates as a single decree rather than separate decrees. That is, the five mandates—be fruitful, multiply, fill the earth, subdue it, and have dominion—are a composite that connects humanity to their world. With that inalterable connection, it is only natural that God should meet his human creatures and that they should meet God in the fabric of that world.

God's Calls to Engagement and Accountability (Gen. 3)

In the Genesis story we see that the Holy Spirit has ordered the narrative to point us forward and deeper into the biblical revelation. That is, when the Lord God comes walking in the garden, the narrative enlarges the picture of the divine-human relationship, as the Lord God anticipates an encounter with the errant human couple and asks, "Where are you?" (Gen. 3:10). This first question signals the fact that God wants to be in a relationship with his human subjects, even though he knows they are hiding from him. It is the story of God seeking humanity, a parable that stretches across the expanse of the biblical story and becomes both the tragedy of humanity's fallen dilemma and the ecstasy of God's compelling love.

At the very outset of the biblical story, God encounters his human creatures at the point of their vulnerability. The attraction to the tree of the knowledge of good and evil involves the human attributes of sight, rationality, and desire, a reflection of God's own image. The divine-human encounter has begun,

6. See chap. 3, "Thinking Comprehensively about God's Goodness (*Tob*)."

and an inherent component of this relationship is accountability, already suggested by the Lord God's prohibition regarding the fruit. These divine questions and their human responses are testimony to the fact that God meets us in the fabric of our world.

The Fabric of the World in the Psalter

A Two-Perspective World

All who espouse a commitment to the biblical faith, even those who may live on the edge of such a commitment, must acknowledge that biblical faith exhibits a vertical/horizontal perspective to which all believers must subscribe. That is, we live in a world that God created and governs, the vertical perspective, and we must relate to him whether we want to or not. The Lord Jesus reminded us of this two-perspective world, the vertical *and* horizontal, in Matthew 22:37–40: "You shall love the Lord your God with all your heart and with all your soul and with all your mind. This is the great and first commandment. And a second is like it: You shall love your neighbor as yourself. On these two commandments depend all the Law and the Prophets" (see Deut. 6:5 and Lev. 19:18).

When we observe this two-perspective worldview, we cannot ignore the Creator or humanity, and we must come to an understanding of how these perspectives work together. In the Lord Jesus's great commandments, the undergirding assumption is that God established this two-perspective view of reality as the operative principle of human life. Even when the Psalms appear to make an exception and admit the existence of those who deny there is a God (Pss. 10:4; 14:1; 53:1), the atheistic statement that "there is no God" may be a practical atheism rather than a theological one. That is, the speakers confess the worldview by which they practically lived. The only legitimate approach to reality is in relationship to God and humankind. In Leviticus 19, where the "love your neighbor" command is found, it is woven into a series of instructions that assure the neighbors' physical survival, protects their property and reputation, assures them a fair wage, pledges them justice in the courts, and so on, and it punctuates these legal assurances with Yahweh's theological pronouncement, "I am the LORD/I am the LORD your God," eleven times in the chapter (e.g., vv. 4, 10, 14, 16). Faith in Yahweh and loving one's neighbors are key parts of a worldview to which believers are committed.

The Fabric of the World in Psalm 99

I would insist that the Psalter, as much as and even more than any other book of the Old Testament, is the maximal illustration of this theological principle. Psalm 99, for example, begins by establishing the undisputed authority of Yahweh, beautifully embracing the vertical/horizontal perspective: "The LORD reigns; let the peoples tremble! He sits enthroned upon the cherubim; let the earth quake! The LORD is great in Zion; he is exalted over all the peoples. Let them praise your great and awesome name! Holy is he!" (vv. 1–3).

Once the sovereign Lord's majesty and authority are established, capped by his unique and inimitable being—"Holy is he!" (Ps. 99:3; cf. Lev. 19)—our psalmist begins to describe the practical side of God's involvement in our world. God executes justice: "The King in his might loves justice. You have established equity; you have executed justice and righteousness in Jacob" (v. 4; cf. Lev. 19). To illustrate the judicial system by which the heavenly King operates, the suppliant of Psalm 99 gives an example of how God relates to Moses, Aaron, and Samuel. When they called on the Lord, he answered them; he portrays himself as a "forgiving God" and an "avenger" of wrongdoings (v. 6), an allusion to the two-sided nature of God portrayed in the second Sinai covenant (Exod. 34:6–7). God is a self-respecting God and demands the loyalty of his followers. Psalm 99 weaves together the Lord's holiness (vv. 3, 5, 9) and his justice, suggesting that holiness is the fountain of his justice. Immediately after the psalmist acclaims the Lord's justice (v. 4), he bids the peoples[7] to worship him and then crowns the summons with the declaration that he is holy: "Exalt the LORD our God; worship at his footstool! Holy is he!" (v. 5).

The Fabric of the World in Psalm 146

Psalm 146 is another beautiful expression of our meeting God in the fabric of the world, or the fact that God, who takes the initiative, meets us there. Verses 6–9 of this psalm echo the divine care that Psalm 8 declares God lavishes on us human beings. David exults in the Lord "who made heaven and earth" (146:5–6) and then enumerates the great works he executes in the world. He executes justice, feeds the hungry, sets the prisoners free, opens the blinded eyes, lifts up those who have fallen, watches over the sojourners, upholds the widow and the fatherless, and brings the wicked to ruin. It is of extraordinary

---

7. The Hebrew verbs are plural and evidently address "all the peoples," including Israel.

importance that both Psalm 146 and Psalm 8, along with many others, put God's work of creation alongside the doctrine of divine providence. This psalm of praise does it as splendidly as any of the psalms: "Blessed is he whose help is the God of Jacob, whose hope is in the LORD his God, who made heaven and earth, the sea, and all that is in them" (146:5–6).

When we human beings are overcome with a false sense of inferiority, these words of Psalm 146, like those of Psalm 8, can serve as a corrective. It is in our world that we meet our Creator and recognize that we are touched by his tender and fashioning fingers. This theological undergirding in the Psalms is a comforting reminder of God's condescension. While the Psalms are rife with the evidence and reminder that "we meet God in the fabric of the world," it is only because of the truth in the turn of the phrase: "God meets us in the fabric of the world." And that is all grace!

SIXTEEN

The Fear of the Lord

The Nature of Wisdom and Its Emphases

Our study at this point turns in the direction of wisdom, a subdiscipline of Old Testament theology. Wisdom pervaded the intellectual traditions of the ancient Near East. It was a way of thinking and behaving, characterizing the thoughts and actions of successful leaders of kingdoms and heads of families. Paul House explains it as a way of living well: "Those who learn to operate effectively in the many circumstances that punctuate human existence are considered wise. Those who have and yet are unable or refuse to learn to act wisely are deemed naïve, simple, or Fools."[1]

This way of thinking and acting penetrated the full social spectrum, from kings to commoners. Its presence in the social orders of the ancient world, especially the biblical world, is witnessed in the so-called wisdom books of the Hebrew Bible: Proverbs, Ecclesiastes, and Job. Some would include the Song of Songs, although that book should probably be assigned its own special category. The penetrating effect of wisdom thought is sometimes called a movement, and some scholars even speak in terms of wisdom schools. While there probably were enclaves of people who popularized this style of thought and conduct and had a teacher-student relationship, it was not likely as formal as the prophetic schools that followed certain prophets, like Elijah and Elisha (see, e.g., 1 Kings 20:35–43).

---

1. House, *Old Testament Theology*, 425.

These three wisdom books constitute a collection of literature produced by this movement, King Solomon being its major proprietor in Israel. Even though the movement in its formal structure was a way of thinking and behaving, it permeated the popular culture of the ancient Near East, penetrating language and culture in general. An analogous movement to help us understand the pervasive presence of wisdom thought might be the modern movement toward political correctness. While I find many aspects of political correctness unacceptable, especially when this movement's principles dictate theological and biblical restrictions, it is perhaps still the best illustration of how a movement can penetrate into all aspects of a society. Undeniably, this way of thinking has pervaded every cultural formality in modern America—politics, business, social life, and religion. Its prominent advocates are educational institutions, and its widespread influence in American culture is attributable to the formal and generally well-funded educational systems, as well as the rise of social media. The objection could be raised that the pervasive influence of political correctness in our world is possible only because of our mass communication systems. Even though that certainly helps explain the success of political correctness, we should not underestimate the influence and power of the oral word in the biblical world, despite the absence of these platforms. The masses were often pawns of the monarchical system of governance and the major institutions of ancient Israel: kings, prophets, and priests. The prophetic movement, more than either the kings or the priests, constituted both an affirmative and counteractive force in Israelite society. We, of course, hear more from the counteractive words of the writing prophets than the kings or the priests. Their condemnation of the false prophets, for example, is, for the most part, the only window we have into that movement in ancient Israel. The power of the spoken word in the biblical world was immense.

While we need not elevate wisdom to a worldview, it nevertheless moved in that direction, insisting that the order and movement of nature were a function of God's creative activity and providence. For example, wisdom is characterized by a primary emphasis on Yahweh as Creator rather than Yahweh as Redeemer, as in the prophetic books. At the same time, wisdom does not ignore Yahweh's redeeming power nor the prophets his creating power, but the balance falls more heavily on one doctrine than the other. It may well be the case that to resolve this tension the psalmists often make creation and redemption cohosts of God's actions toward Israel and the world (see chap. 1, "The *Aleph* and *Tav* of Psalmic Theology"). Recall that Psalms is the product of several centuries of Israel's religious thought and worship, so its approach to various topics may reflect centuries of coalescing thoughts rather than conscious editorial decisions.

Further, wisdom tends to simplify Israel's understanding of the religious order, opting for two ways, the way of the wise/righteous and the way of the fool/wicked. Psalm 1 is a good example of this simple classification. Yet, despite these portraits in its introductory psalm, the Psalter does not develop these religious classifications, except in a very general way. That is, the psalmists do not present this two-way theology as the prevailing view of the Psalter. When such a view appears, it is a minor emphasis. Nevertheless, there are hints that the psalmists sometimes want to deflect believers from the wisdom system of thought to the favored psalmic system, meditation on the torah (Ps. 1:2), and this very often translates into recognizing and enjoying the presence of Yahweh (but see my comments on Psalm 119 above). This emphasis is particularly strong in many of the David psalms (e.g., Pss. 16:11; 17:15; 23:6; 27:4); and the final psalm of Book 3 makes a strong case for trusting in Yahweh's steadfast love (*hesed*) even when the covenantal promises to David seem to have languished (Ps. 89). David, particularly in Books 3 and 5, becomes both the exemplar of Yahweh's love and its envoy: "My faithfulness and my steadfast love shall be with him, and in my name shall his horn be exalted" (89:24). The opening psalm of Book 5 offers a final word of commendation that the wise should concentrate on Yahweh's love, perhaps hinting that a transition from wisdom to steadfast love is the theme of Book 5: "Whoever is wise, let him attend to these things; let them consider the steadfast love of the Lord" (107:43). This note resounds in the catchphrase of the opening chapters of Proverbs, repeated in Psalm 111:10: "The fear of the Lord is the beginning of wisdom; all those who practice it have a good understanding. His praise endures forever!" (see Prov. 1:7; 9:10; also Ps. 110:11).

While we should recognize the influence of wisdom thought on the Psalter—a minor influence, I would insist—Psalms 19 and 119 bring to the table an overwhelming emphasis on the torah and its instruction. The Psalter's attention to the temple and worship is evidence that the final shape of the Psalter cannot be attributed to the wisdom sages[2] but is much more likely to

2. See Ceresko, "The Sage in the Psalms," 227–30.

have been due to prophetic and priestly efforts. The covenantal undercurrent, sometimes becoming a rushing stream, represents an effort to establish a collection of prayers and meditations that support the Mosaic covenant, especially the second Sinai covenant (Exod. 34:6–7). Even David, the major figure of the Psalter, becomes a Moses-like character, a true believer in Yahweh's covenant faithfulness (Ps. 86:15).

A Mark of Faith and Practice

Like Christianity, the Old Testament faith has terms to designate those persons who have reached a summit of faith. When the psalmists speak of being in the presence of God, it is the ultimate expression of the journey of faith, only short of seeing the face of God. The more general term in the Old Testament for the journey of faith, which is synonymous with experiencing God's grace, is "the fear of the LORD/God." This is evident especially in the Torah, the wisdom books, and the Psalms. The book of Job is a journal of one man's faith, and it opens with a final assessment of his faith after his many trials and struggles: "That man was blameless and upright, one who feared God and turned away from evil" (Job 1:1). This would have been as appropriate at the end of the book as at its beginning. Indeed, Job 1–2 is a preliminary statement that both introduces Job's piety and hints at the outcome of his struggle of faith.

Those who believed in Yahweh are sometimes called "saints" (*hasidim*), and sometimes God/Yahweh-fearers. The verb *yr'* ("to fear") was the normative term used in this title, either as a finite verb or as a participle. The phrase "the fear of the LORD" was a standard term for unqualified devotion to Yahweh. Job's fear of God was a condition of both his faith ("blameless and upright") and his practice ("turned away from evil"). That is to say, his disposition was one of religious devotion and moral integrity.

Two Kinds of Fear: Mortal and Religious

In the Old Testament, especially as highlighted in the Psalms, there are two kinds of fear. One is the mortal fear we have when we face threatening and frightful circumstances, a fear often expressed with the Hebrew verb *phd*. The other is the fear or awe we experience in the presence of God and his great works in history, expressed with the Hebrew verb *yr'*. In Psalm 27:1 both terms are used synonymously in parallel lines:

> The LORD is my light and my salvation;
>> whom shall I fear [*yr'*]?
> The LORD is the stronghold of my life;
>> of whom shall I be afraid [*phd*]?

The mention of the name Yahweh in verse 1 gives the answer before the question is posed; and based on the military metaphors of salvation (victory), light, and stronghold, the Lord is the only one who can be relied upon and trusted. The parallel verb (*phd*) in the second line is the verb that normally expresses mortal fear but is sometimes used interchangeably with the verb *yr'*. Even here, judging from the military terms, there is a sense of mortal fear, and the content of the psalm supports this idea. David mentions his adversaries, enemies, and foes, but even when they threaten his life and security he does not fear (*phd*), because the Lord is his defender. Obviously the fear of the Lord and mortal fear are not the same emotions, but they can feel the same. The faith that undergirds those who trust in the Lord turns even mortal fear into the fear of the Lord.

The Fear of the Lord and Creation

Knowing the pervasive presence of the doctrine of creation in the Psalms, we are not surprised to find the psalmist declaring that the fear of the Lord is based in Yahweh's creation of the world and his providential care. We must keep in mind also that the world God created is "full of the steadfast love of the LORD," manifested in God's love of "righteousness and justice" (Ps. 33:5). The terms of this text are so close to the language of Genesis 1 that we sense the psalmist knows that text. Yahweh's act of creation is enough to elicit, even demand, that the earth and all its inhabitants fear the Lord.

> He loves righteousness and justice;
>> the earth is full of the steadfast love of the LORD.
>
> By the word of the LORD the heavens were made,
>> and by the breath of his mouth all their host.
> He gathers the waters of the sea as a heap;
>> he puts the deeps in storehouses.

> Let all the earth fear [*yr'*] the LORD;
>> let all the inhabitants of the world stand in awe of him!
> For he spoke, and it came to be;
>> he commanded, and it stood firm. (Ps. 33:5–9)

Even with their limited knowledge of the world, the ancients stood in awe of the Lord. With our vast knowledge of the universe, which is yet in its infancy, our awe of the Creator should be indescribably immense.

The Proper Posture of Worship

The spirit in which we worship the Lord is of utmost importance. Jesus spoke to this concern and gave us a directive: "But the hour is coming, and is now here, when the true worshipers will worship the Father in spirit and truth, for the Father is seeking such people to worship him" (John 4:23). Given the worship quality that pervades the Psalms, it is not surprising that they provide an antecedent to this worship posture that the Lord Jesus lays down for his people. In Psalm 2 we receive a watchword for the entire book: "Serve the LORD with fear" (2:11). The verb "serve" (*'bd*) carries the sense of "worship," as it does in Psalm 100:2, "Serve the LORD with gladness!" David expresses this spirit of worship more clearly in Psalm 5:7: "I will bow down toward your holy temple in the fear of you." And the benefits of grace accrue when the worshiper maintains this deportment: Yahweh becomes the instructor (25:12); the worshipers become recipients of his goodness (31:19); the Lord's watchful eye is always upon them (33:18); and even the angels encamp around those who fear the Lord (34:7).

The Fear of the Lord and God's Steadfast Love

The steadfast love of God and the fear of the Lord are bound in a unique relationship. The fear of the Lord is the medium and the steadfast love of God is the end. Those who fear the Lord discover, expressed spatially, its inestimable proportions: "For as high as the heavens are above the earth, so great is his steadfast love toward those who fear him" (Ps. 103:11). Put in terms of time and eternity, "the steadfast love [*hesed*] of the LORD is from everlasting to everlasting on those who fear him, and his righteousness to children's children" (v. 17). It follows that the appropriation of the steadfast love of God, what Paul called "the unsearchable riches of Christ" (Eph. 3:8), is attainable only through the medium of the fear of the Lord.

The Fear of the Lord and the Covenant

The fear of the Lord is an instrument of grace that leads us in the direction of the covenant, at least as laid out in Book 5. I have already made the point that the second Sinai covenant (Exod. 34:6–7) is the prevailing form of the covenant in the Psalter. Collected against the backdrop of Israel's miraculous return from exile, restoration to their homeland, and the reinstitution of worship in Jerusalem, Book 5 is a religious journal of a nation on the path again to learning the fear of the Lord. Lest the emphasis escape us, we should note that the two introductory psalms to the Egyptian Hallel remind us of the alliance between Yahweh's steadfast love and the second Sinai covenant (Pss. 111–12). The occurrence of two key terms from the Sinai covenant constitutes an allusion to Exodus 34:6: the Lord is "merciful" and "gracious" (*rahum* and *hannun*). Further, the psalm assures us that the Lord's covenant is eternal: "He remembers his covenant forever" (Ps. 111:5); and "He has commanded his covenant forever" (v. 9). Now, in this critical time of transition from exile to freedom, the psalmist hints that this most recent work of God is linked to all of the Almighty's great works in Israel's history, recalling his majestic work of grace that spared his erring people under Moses. In fact, the Lord has "sent redemption to his people" (v. 9), reminding them of that momentous covenant on Sinai:

> Great are the works of the LORD,
>   studied by all who delight in them.
> Full of splendor and majesty is his work,
>   and his righteousness endures forever.
> He has caused his wondrous works to be remembered;
>   the LORD is *gracious* and *merciful*. (Ps. 111:2–4)

The psalm later picks up a thread that has already appeared in Psalm 111:5 ("He provides food for *those who fear him*; he remembers his covenant forever") and assures the Lord's redeemed people that the fear of the Lord is a means for understanding Yahweh's wonderful works and his trustworthy precepts (see v. 7).

I am working with the idea that the Egyptian Hallel (Pss. 113–18, with Pss. 111–12 functioning as an introduction) has the grand design of making Psalm 119 the capstone of its momentous celebration of God's great works. In so doing, the literary designer promotes the doctrine of the fear of the Lord as the catalyst that leads to understanding God's wonderful works in history, especially the first and second exoduses. I realize the temptation to see inclusios everywhere in the Psalms, but it is hard to ignore the fact that Psalm 111 ends with the motto of wisdom:

> The fear of the LORD is the beginning of wisdom;
>> all those who practice it have a good understanding.
> His praise endures forever! (Ps. 111:10)

Further, a string of references to the fear of the Lord runs through the Egyptian Hallel (Pss. 111:5, 10; 112:1; 115:11, 13; 118:4), and Psalm 119 culminates this liturgical document with ample similar references (119:38, 63, 74, 79, 120). My proposal is that the fear of the Lord is a means for restoring Israel to spiritual health after the long and life-threatening exile in Babylonia. That is, the restoration movement after the exile needed theological instruments to encourage the advancement of the new life, and the fear of the Lord, attached to the instrument of torah, was the major instrument of grace the writer of Psalm 119 was setting forth. Elsewhere I have made a case for the formula of grace (Exod. 34:6–7) being that instrument.[3] The fear of the Lord is both the catalyst to a new life through the torah and the end product of that new life, celebrated in Psalm 119.

Casting Our Faith in the Personae of Those Who Fear the Lord

The fear of the Lord is a timeless posture of faith. We have already seen how the psalmists sometimes cast one persona in the character of other notable figures of Israel's history, like Abraham, Joshua, and Moses. Christianity has taken its cue from Scripture and made this a standard hermeneutical practice. Preachers and teachers generally assume they are authorized to do the same, and so they are! Yet, while this study of the Psalms has taken liberties with theological applications, liberties that the Psalms themselves practice and

3. Bullock, "Covenant Renewal and the Formula of Grace."

endorse, we should be cautious not to overinterpret these poems of grace and beauty. At the same time, we are authorized by the psalmists' own application of these hermeneutical principles to replicate them in our own lives. This is, in fact, one of the internal powers of the Psalms.

Speaking from my own observations, I believe the idea of the fear of the Lord as a spiritual posture that leads and directs us into a deeper relationship with Christ is a spiritual motivator of great merit. In our world where spiritual things are sometimes mocked and often degraded to attitudes that only the unsophisticated readers of Scripture would espouse, there is an appropriate spirit in which we should approach our God in worship and represent him in practice. For example, humility is one aspect of fearing God, and one that all readers of Scripture should pray for. Calvin reminds us that there are two kinds of knowledge, the knowledge of God and the knowledge of ourselves.[4] Both kinds should be sought and both acquired alongside each other. A knowledge of ourselves without the knowledge of God will turn us into idolators, while a knowledge of God without the knowledge of ourselves will create a spiritual person who knows nothing of the incarnation—God became man and dwelt among us.

And Paul admonishes us to be of the same mind as Christ Jesus (Phil. 2:5–11) and says the goal of this posture of faith is "that I may know him and the power of his resurrection, and may share his sufferings, becoming like him in his death" (3:10). This is to know God in his highest revelation in Jesus Christ, and at the same time to know God by taking up our cross and following Jesus, suffering with and for our Savior. Whatever spiritual persona among the ancients we might find comfortable, the One that we seek, the One to which all others point, is that of Jesus Christ, that we might become like him. This is the spiritual posture of the New Testament church as they began to grow in their knowledge of Christ: "So the church throughout all Judea and Galilee and Samaria had peace and was being built up. And walking in *the fear of the Lord* and in the comfort of the Holy Spirit, it multiplied" (Acts 9:31).

---

4. Calvin, *Institutes of the Christian Religion*, 1:35.

SEVENTEEN

Praise of God, the Rehearsal Hall for Eternity

Orienting from Time to Eternity

When we think of eternal life, one of our questions is how we will occupy ourselves during an unending life. Our activities in this world are time oriented, dominated, in fact, by time—time saved, time passed, time wasted, time that passed too quickly. The first part of the answer to our question is that we, by the very nature of eternality, will be reoriented to the absence of time. In our present world we can only imagine the implications of this reorientation to eternity. John gives us a picture of the church symbolized by the 144,000, "the ones coming out of the great tribulation. They have washed their robes and made them white in the blood of the Lamb. Therefore they are before the throne of God, and serve him day and night in his temple; and he who sits on the throne will shelter them with his presence" (Rev. 7:14–15). Then comes John's hint of the reorientation:

> They shall hunger no more, neither thirst anymore;
> > the sun shall not strike them,
> > nor any scorching heat.
> For the Lamb in the midst of the throne will be their shepherd,
> > and he will guide them to springs of living water,
> and God will wipe away every tear from their eyes. (Rev. 7:16–17)

John describes reorientation in terms of the cessation of those natural phenomena that can be so troublesome, like the sun's heat and resulting thirst,
and he adds the detail that the new creation will be distinguished by the
presence of Christ, the Lamb, who will be our Shepherd. But those are still
the bare details, and the rest is left to our imagination.

Most importantly, the central feature of John's description of eternity is that
he centers his message upon Jesus Christ. In a sense he is filling out the details
of the place that Christ has gone to prepare for us (see John 14). The picture
of the "multitude that no one could number" who have "washed their robes
and made them white in the blood of the Lamb" (Rev. 7:9, 14) is a statement
regarding the church's presence in heaven. The revelator sees another scene that
sheds more light on the 144,000: "And they were singing a new song before the
throne and before the four living creatures and before the elders. No one could
learn that song except the 144,000 who had been redeemed from the earth"
(Rev. 14:3). This "new song" reminds us of the instances in the Psalter when
a new age or a new event is introduced and celebrated with a "new song."[1]
Further, Peter makes a captivating comment on the mysteries of our glorious
redemption, that they are "things into which the angels long to look" (1 Pet.
1:12). The very presence of the church in heaven redeemed by the blood of the
Lamb and eternally praising God is such a magnificent truth, but one which
naturally challenges our imagination. We will be preoccupied by praising God
and will never tire of rehearsing redemption's story and the mysteries of love.

The Eternal Praise of God in Heaven

To speak of the nature of praising God is audacious because we will probably
learn ways to praise God in eternity that we have not even dreamed about in
our world. Yet, this world is our rehearsal hall, where we can prepare ourselves
for the eternal praise of God, and the Psalms are our maestro as we listen to,
repeat, and repeat again God's praises as recorded in the Psalter. In fact, in
the present we have the opportunity to develop a regimen of thanksgiving and
praise that will certainly exercise and strengthen our spiritual vocal cords for
heaven. Richard Baxter says, "Bend your soul to study eternity; busy it about
the life to come; habituate yourself to such contemplations, and let not those
thoughts be seldom and cursory, but settle upon them; dwell here and bathe

1. Pss. 33:3; 40:3; 96:1; 98:1; 149:1; cf. Rev. 5:9; 14:3. See also Bullock, *Psalms*, 2:542–43.

your soul in heaven's delights . . . until you have got some mastery over them, you will then find yourself in the suburbs of heaven."[2]

Declarative Praise

The Psalms engage in two kinds of praises, declarative and descriptive.[3] Declarative praise attributes glory and honor to God by its mere words, such as the expressions "Praise the LORD" and "Bless the LORD." The psalmists give us practice in the discipline of the language of praise. An American missionary, speaking of the wonder of language, said that when he learned Spanish he discovered that he could say things in Spanish he could not say in English; and when he learned the language of the indigenous people who were his target ministry, he could say things in their language that he couldn't say in Spanish. That reminds me of the psalms that tutor us in the language of praise. Some psalms incorporate language of praise that surpasses other psalms of praise. Psalm 103 is a psalm of praise *par excellence*, but we should not expect all other psalms to achieve its beauty and clarity; there are degrees of literary beauty and theological acuteness in the psalms. This does not diminish the importance of any psalms; rather, it recognizes the beauty of their differences, and that is something to celebrate.

In the course of time, the psalmists came to employ the superlative term of praise, "hallelujah" ("Praise the LORD"). I propose, judging from the exclusive use of "hallelujah" in Books 4 and 5 of the Psalter and chapter 19 of Revelation, that "hallelujah" was intended as the supreme word of praise in the temple. Whether or not this is the case, it is still true that the praise language of the Psalms advances in stages. And heaven, we can safely assume, will continue our earthly education in the praise of God—existential to the fullest extent—as we and the redeemed of the ages grow in God-honoring language. C. S. Lewis speaks of this spiritual phenomenon: "If it were possible for a created soul fully . . . to 'appreciate,' that is to love and delight in, the worthiest object of all, and simultaneously at every moment to give this delight perfect expression, then that soul would be in supreme beatitude. It is along these lines that I find it easiest to understand the Christian doctrine that 'Heaven' is a state in which angels now, and men hereafter, are perpetually employed in praising God."[4]

2. Baxter, *The Saints' Everlasting Rest*, 484.
3. See "The Language of Creation" in chap. 1.
4. Lewis, *Reflections on the Psalms*, 96.

"Supreme beatitude" sounds like a welcome posture for eternity! What Charles Spurgeon says of the Psalter's concluding psalms of praise (Pss. 146–50) may be extended to the eternal order of redemption: "The flow of the broad river of the Book of Psalms ends in a cataract of praise."[5] Psalms 146–50 constitute the summit of praise in the Psalter, as we hear all creation praising the Lord. To John the revelator the eternal praise of God sounded like a multitude of voices, and twice in Revelation 19 John hears the praises of God wafting from the portals of heaven and calls them the loud "voice of a great multitude" (Rev. 19:1, 6). Then the revelator amends the report to say "like the roar of many waters and like the sound of mighty peals of thunder" (v. 6). The scene is one of unspeakable awe and mystery as earth's redeemed and heaven's choral magistrates join their voices to announce the marriage supper of the Lamb. Christ and his church have now become one in the unbreakable bond of God's redeeming love. Our Savior's prayer for unity is answered (John 17). The words are not forced but rise easily and joyfully from the finished work of Christ: "Let us rejoice and exult and give him the glory, for the marriage of the Lamb has come, and his Bride has made herself ready" (Rev. 19:7).

Katherine Hankey captures so beautifully the joy of this new song in her poem set to music by William Fischer, the hymn "I Love to Tell the Story." The hymn proclaims that every time we tell that story in our world it is more wonderfully sweet, and those who know it best are "hungering and thirsting" to hear it like the rest—we never tire of its tones and overtones! Thankfully the motivation is true for believers in the rehearsal hall for eternity, and Hankey even applies her testimony to eternity itself:

> I love to tell the story—
> 'Tis pleasant to repeat
> What seems, each time I tell it,
> More wonderfully sweet;
> I love to tell the story—
> For some have never heard
> The message of salvation
> From God's own holy Word.
>
> I love to tell the story—
> For those who know it best

---

5. Spurgeon, *Treasury of David*, 3:414 (on Ps. 147:1).

> Seem hungering and thirsting
> To hear it like the rest;
> And when in scenes of glory
> I sing the new, new song,
> 'Twill be the old, old story,
> That I have loved so long.

This is the story that no one but the redeemed can sing, so let us engage in tuning our voices to the language of the Psalms and other biblical praises, preparing ourselves for what may be only the beginners' choir in heaven.

Descriptive Praise

The descriptive praise of God in the Psalms and elsewhere in Scripture is constituted by portrayals of what God has done, including the day-to-day experiences of God's goodness appropriated by individuals. Declarative praise can be intermeshed with descriptive praise. When the psalmist says, "Come and hear, all you who fear God, and I will tell you what he has done for me" (Ps. 66:16), he engages in descriptive praise. Psalm 66 is characterized by this praise, except for one instance of declarative praise ("Blessed be God," v. 20).

In John's vision of heaven, the redeemed are the grateful recipients of the sacrificial sufficiency of the Lamb who shed his precious blood, by which their lives were transformed. The story of redemption has reached its triumphant conclusion. The tension between good and evil has been left behind, with its suffering and tears. So the descriptive praise of heaven, whatever details it may involve, will be drastically different from the descriptive praise of the Psalter. It will indeed be a flowing stream of "what God has done for us." Redemption's story will have met the standard of God's kingdom and kingdom citizens: "Your kingdom come, *your will be done, on earth as it is in heaven*" (Matt. 6:10). Authentic praise of God can be rendered only by authentic citizens of the kingdom who do God's authentic will.[6]

But there is something more that we ought to acclaim. The very presence of the redeemed in the presence of God will be a major declaration of God's love—descriptive praise of God. While verbal praise will resound throughout eternity, just the presence of the redeemed will bespeak the victory of the cross and the glory of the resurrection. God created humankind in his image, and in

6. Bullock, *Psalms*, 2:133.

heaven the redeemed will have been conformed to Christ's image, to use Paul's language. When we look in each other's faces we will see the resemblance of Jesus. John's way of saying this is that they have washed their robes in the blood of the Lamb; they are the indisputable evidence of the sufficiency of Christ's blood, and that evidence will redound to the glory of God—praise without words. The use of words, of course, will tell forth the redemption story, sung only by the redeemed, and the very presence of the redeemed around the throne of God will be the sweet and wordless refrain of Christ's redeeming love, much like the heavens declare (Pss. 19:1; 65:8). What God planned from the foundation of the world will have been accomplished, and earth and heaven will sing a new song. Just think, you and I will be members of that immortal and eternal choir and never tire of singing God's praises. Our songs of praise will be inexpressibly lovely, as will our redeemed presence. Hallelujah!

BIBLIOGRAPHY

Augustine. *The Confessions of St. Augustine*. Translated by Rex Warner. New York: New American Library, 1963.

The Babylonian Talmud. Edited by I. Epstein. London: Soncino, 1948. https://archive .org/details/TheBabylonianTalmudcompleteSoncinoEnglishTranslation.

Bainton, Roland H. *Here I Stand: A Life of Martin Luther*. Nashville: Abingdon, 1960.

Baxter, Richard. *The Saints' Everlasting Rest*. Fearn, Ross-shire: Christian Focus, 1998.

Beale, G. K. *We Become What We Worship: A Biblical Theology of Idolatry*. Downers Grove, IL: IVP Academic, 2008.

Bechtel, Lyn M. "Shame as a Sanction of Social Control in Biblical Israel: Judicial, Political, and Social Shaming." *Journal for the Study of the Old Testament* 49 (1991): 47–76.

Bullock, C. Hassell. "Covenant Renewal and the Formula of Grace in the Psalter." *Bibliotheca Sacra* 170 (2019): 18–34.

———. *Encountering the Book of Psalms*. 2nd ed. Grand Rapids: Baker Academic, 2018.

———. "Excavating the 'Fossil Record' of a Metaphor: The Use of the Verb *nasa'* as 'to Forgive' in the Psalter." In *Reading the Psalms Theologically*, edited by David Howard Jr. and Andrew Schmutzer, 127–40. Bellingham, WA: Lexham, 2023.

———. *Psalms*. 2 vols. Teach the Text Commentary Series. Grand Rapids: Baker Books, 2015–17.

———. "Psalms, Book of." In *Dictionary of the New Testament Use of the Old Testament*, edited by G. K. Beale, D. A. Carson, Benjamin L. Gladd, and Andrew David Naselli. Grand Rapids: Baker Academic, 2023.

Calvin, John. *Commentaries on the Book of Genesis*. 2 vols. Translated by John King. Reprint. Grand Rapids: Baker Books, 2003.

————. *Commentary on the Book of Psalms.* 5 vols. Reprint. Grand Rapids: Baker, 1979.

————. *Concerning Scandals.* Translated by John W. Fraser. Grand Rapids: Eerdmans, 1978.

————. *Institutes of the Christian Religion.* 2 vols. Edited by John T. McNeill. Translated by Ford Lewis Battles. Louisville: Westminster, 1960.

Ceresko, Anthony R. "The Sage in the Psalms." In *The Sage in Israel and the Ancient Near East,* edited by John G. Gammie and Leo G. Perdue, 217–30. Winona Lake, IN: Eisenbrauns, 1990.

Chesterton, G. K. *Orthodoxy.* Garden City, NY: Doubleday, 1959.

Cross, Frank Moore. *Canaanite Myth and Hebrew Epic: Essays in the History of the Religion of Israel.* Cambridge: Harvard University Press, 1973.

Delitzsch, Franz. *Biblical Commentary on the Psalms.* 3 vols. London: Hodder & Stoughton, 1888–94.

Forsyth, P. T. *The Soul of Prayer.* 1916. Reprint. Vancouver: Regent College Publishing, 2002.

Gerstenberger, Erhard S. *Psalms.* Part 1. Grand Rapids: Eerdmans, 1988.

Glueck, Nelson. Ḥesed *in the Bible.* Translated by Alfred Gottschalk. Cincinnati: Hebrew Union College Press, 1967.

Gruber, Mayer I. *Rashi's Commentary on the Psalms.* Brill Reference Library of Judaism 18. Leiden: Brill, 2004.

Gunkel, Hermann. *Introduction to Psalms: The Genres of the Religious Lyric of Israel.* Translated by James D. Nogalski. Macon, GA: Mercer University Press, 1998.

————. *The Psalms: A Form-Critical Introduction.* Philadelphia: Fortress, 1967.

Hakham, Amos. *The Bible: Psalms with the Jerusalem Commentary.* 3 vols. Jerusalem: Mosad Harav Kook, 2003.

Hankey, Katherine. "I Love to Tell the Story." In *The Covenant Hymnal,* no. 530. Chicago: Covenant Press, 1973.

Hays, Richard B. *Echoes of Scripture in the Letters of Paul.* New Haven: Yale University Press, 1989.

The Heidelberg Catechism. Christian Reformed Church (website). Accessed January 3, 2023. https://www.crcna.org/welcome/beliefs/confessions/heidelberg-catechism.

Hensley, Adam D. *Covenant Relationships and the Editing of the Hebrew Psalter.* London: T&T Clark, 2018.

Hossfeld, Frank-Lothar, and Eric Zenger. *Psalms 3: A Commentary on the Psalms 101–151.* Hermeneia. Minneapolis: Fortress, 2011.

House, Paul R. *Old Testament Theology.* Downers Grove, IL: InterVarsity, 1998.

Kidner, Derek. *Psalms 1–72.* Tyndale Old Testament Commentaries. Downers Grove, IL: InterVarsity, 1975.

———. *Psalms 73–150*. Tyndale Old Testament Commentaries. Downers Grove, IL: InterVarsity, 1975.

Kuyper, Abraham. *To Be Near unto God*. Classic Domain Publishing, n.d.

Lewis, C. S. *Reflections on the Psalms*. London: Geoffrey Bles, 1958.

Lowell, James Russell. "The Present Crisis." Poets.org. Accessed December 12, 2022. https://poets.org/poem/present-crisis.

MacDonald, George. *Thomas Wingfold, Curate*. Toronto: Copp, Clark & Co., 1876.

Mays, James Luther. *The Lord Reigns: A Theological Handbook to the Psalms*. Louisville: Westminster John Knox, 1994.

Moule, C. F. D. *The Meaning of Hope*. Philadelphia: Fortress, 1963.

Mowinckel, Sigmund. *He That Cometh*. Translated by G. W. Anderson. Oxford: Blackwell, 1959.

———. *The Psalms in Israel's Worship*. 2 vols. Translated by D. R. Ap-Thomas. Oxford: Blackwell, 1962.

North, Frank Mason. "Where Cross the Crowded Ways of Life." In *Hymns for Praise and Worship*, no. 278. Napanee, IN: Evangel Press, 1984.

Parrott, Thomas Marc. Introduction to *The First Part of Henry the Fourth*. In *Twenty-Three Plays and the Sonnets*, by William Shakespeare, 349–85. Rev. ed. New York: Scribner's Sons, 1953.

Pattison, Bonnie L. "The Suffering Church in Calvin's *De Scandalis*: An Exercise in Luther's *Theologia Crucis*?" In *Since We Are Justified by Faith: Justification in the Theologies of the Protestant Reformation*, edited by Michael Parsons, 117–37. Milton Keynes, UK: Paternoster, 2012.

Perowne, J. J. Stewart. *The Book of Psalms*. 2 vols. London: George Bell, 1883.

Peterson, Eugene. *A Long Obedience in the Same Direction: Discipleship in an Instant Society*. Downers Grove, IL: InterVarsity, 1980.

Selderhuis, Herman J. *Calvin's Theology of the Psalms*. Grand Rapids: Baker Academic, 2007.

———. *John Calvin: A Pilgrim's Life*. Trans. Albert Gootjes. Downers Grove, IL: IVP Academic, 2009.

Spieckermann, Hermann. *Gottes Liebe zu Israel*. Studien zur Theologie des Alten Testaments. Tübingen: Mohr Siebeck, 2004.

Spurgeon, Charles. *The Treasury of David*. 3 vols. Reprint. Peabody, MA: Hendrickson, 2011.

Unger, Melvin P. *Handbook to Bach's Sacred Cantata Texts: An Interlinear Translation with Reference Guide to Biblical Quotations and Allusions*. Lanham, MD: Scarecrow, 1996.

Vos, Johannes G. "The Ethical Problem of the Imprecating Psalms." *Westminster Theological Journal* 4 (1992): 123–38.

Weiser, Artur. *Psalms: A Commentary*. Old Testament Library. Philadelphia: Westminster, 1962.

Wesley, Charles. "Love Divine, All Loves Excelling." In *The Covenant Hymnal*, no. 431. Chicago: Covenant Press, 1973.

Westcott, Brooke Foss. *The Epistle to the Hebrews*. New York: Macmillan, 1908.

Wilson, Gerald Henry. *The Editing of the Hebrew Psalter*. Chico, CA: Scholars Press, 1985.

———. *Psalms*. Vol. 1. NIV Application Commentary. Grand Rapids: Zondervan, 2002.

Wordsworth, William. "Ode to Duty." Poetry Foundation. Accessed December 12, 2022. https://www.poetryfoundation.org/poems/45535/ode-to-duty.

Wright, N. T. *The Case for the Psalms: Why They Are Essential*. New York: HarperCollins, 2013.

Zenger, Eric. *A God of Vengeance? Understanding the Psalms of Divine Wrath*. Translated by Linda M. Maloney. Louisville: Westminster John Knox, 1996.

SCRIPTURE INDEX

SUBJECT INDEX